Just Kiss Me and Tell Me You Did the Laundry

Just Kiss Me and Tell Me You Did the Laundry

*How to Negotiate Equal Roles for Husband and
Wife in Parenting, Career, and Home Life*

Karen Bouris

RODALE

© 2004 by Karen Bouris

Printed in the United States of America

Rodale Inc. makes every effort to use acid-free ∞, recycled paper ♻.

Book design by Christina Gaugler

Library of Congress Cataloging-in-Publication Data

Bouris, Karen, date.
    Just kiss me and tell me you did the laundry : how to negotiate equal roles for husband and wife in parenting, career, and home life / Karen Bouris.
        p.   cm.
    Includes bibliographical references and index.
    ISBN 1–57954–760–5 paperback
    1. Households.   2. Sexual division of labor.   3. Housekeeping.
    4. Parenting.   5. Work and family.   I. Title.
    HQ734.B743   2004
    306.3'615—dc22   2003025306

Distributed to the book trade by St. Martin's Press

2   4   6   8   10   9   7   5   3   1   paperback

RODALE

WE **INSPIRE** AND **ENABLE** PEOPLE TO IMPROVE
THEIR LIVES AND THE WORLD AROUND THEM

FOR MORE OF OUR PRODUCTS
WWW.RODALESTORE.COM
(800) 848-4735

To my family

Contents

Introduction

"Never doubt that a small group of thoughtful,
committed citizens can change the world; indeed,
it's the only thing that ever has."

—Margaret Mead

I lay in the dark quiet of our bedroom unable to sleep. My mind was reeling with the books and studies I'd read and stories from women I'd interviewed. I was finally imagining the structure of this book and the possibilities for my own life: one in which happy children, great parenting, a highly developed self, and a fabulous marriage would flow naturally from the changes I was prepared to initiate. Although it was late on a Sunday night, I knew my husband, Gill, lying beside me, was still awake. Unable to contain myself, I began to talk about the book, our relationship, and how if we were partners in making equal parenting a priority, it would be better for our children, our marriage, and society at large.

Pregnant with our second child, you would think I would have figured much of this out already, but it wasn't the case. You might also question my lack of strategy bringing up such a complex and sensitive issue late Sunday night, while lying in bed. As I listed off the benefits of him working less—a 3- or 4-day workweek, for example—and threw out one idea after another, I knew he was listening but was also aware that he was growing more troubled. Abruptly, Gill sprang out of bed and began pacing the room: "Let me just understand these global changes you're wanting to make in our relationship and the world," he said. "Right now, I have all the pressure of earning enough money to support this family—which is difficult in these times, to say the least—yet you're asking me to work less. So now I have the pressure to make more money *and* stay home with our children!?" Silently, I thought, "Yes! You now have the pressure that I and other women have—to financially contribute, run a perfect household, and raise spectacular children." To say he was agitated is an understatement.

As I listened, though, I tried to understand and have compassion for the pressures he felt. In the past, I had been an equal financial partner—sometimes the bigger breadwinner—yet now we were in a situation where I had no regular income, because I was focusing on writing this book while expecting our second baby. He was bearing the entire responsibility for our finances, knowing that I might not have any income for almost a year, during a time of economic recession. Calming down, he got back in bed and put his arms around me.

"I know what the key to your book is," he stated.

"You do?"

"It's men. How willing we are to question old roles and accept new roles. Whether our egos can handle it, and whether we can let go of a lifetime of expectations that no longer fit us."

This was ironic, I thought, for I believed the key was for *women* to expect more, to insist on the changes they wanted and needed in their relationships in order to manifest intentional parenting roles.

What motivation did men have to change the status quo, after all? They didn't yet know what was to be gained. But here was my husband saying that it was his responsibility—men's responsibility—to change their mindset, to reject or expand the male role models with which they'd grown up. He pointed out that men were trapped in their own gender roles—accustomed to measuring their success and "manhood" with dollar signs, competing with each other and in the rigid role of provider—and that this was no picnic.

As he continued, I realized the sweeping implications of my proposal. Taking intentional steps toward equal parenting would require many shifts and changes: women insisting on change and men's willingness to accept and embrace their new roles; men letting go of their attachment to the breadwinner role and women letting go of the idea of being taken care of; women accepting equal responsibility for finances and men accepting equal responsibility for child care and housework; men opening their hearts to their children and the women in their lives; and women loosening their grip on control and status as the number-one parent.

I share this personal story to illustrate that I am fully aware of how difficult it is to balance work and family and intentional parenting roles. Like parents everywhere, I struggle to make it all work. Sometimes I think I'm a fabulous mother and have made great choices for myself and my family: I read the right books, am engaged with my children, have a relatively organized house, and am personally fulfilled with my work and external life. More frequently, though, I judge myself as a hot-and-cold mother, sometimes not very fabulous at all. I feel guilty, then resentful of the guilt, then guilty about feeling resentful—a pointless emotional cycle that some mothers know well.

The minute I had children, my heart grew a new chamber—a sacred space holding a new love source, pumping deeply and elaborately inside. Yet I felt dissatisfaction, not with mothering, but with the assumptions around parenting, particularly mothering. I found myself angry at the double standards for good mothers versus good fathers. I was angry at a society that accepted this as the norm and frustrated with other women who had bought into the program that it is our biological destiny (and ours alone) to give up our lives and devote ourselves to our families. I was angry at policies and institutions that didn't value parenthood. And I was upset with my husband, who more or less kept on with his life while my life was turned upside down. Questions ran through my head: What was so wrong with wanting my husband to be my equal partner? Didn't it make perfect sense that two parents should love and raise their children together? Why was everyone okay with marriages that were suffering and even acrimonious? Wasn't I giving my children a better role model and a happier parent if I was passionately engaged in my own work life? Isn't a stable, loving marriage—one based on equality—the best environment I can provide for my children?

Luckily, my anger mellowed and the questions clarified. I discovered that everywhere I turned—in the park, at my moms' groups, on radio and television talk shows—I heard people asking their own versions of similar questions. At the same time, my book group, most of us mothers working at least part-time, read *The Price of Motherhood*, a groundbreaking book by Ann Crittenden detailing why motherhood is still devalued in our culture. We were up in arms! We wanted to enact change in our places of work, in our communities, and in public policy. In the same breath though, we complained that we couldn't even get our husbands to pick the kids up from school once a week, help with our children's doctor appointments, or pitch in around the house. It seemed overwhelming. Surely, we would have difficulty changing policy and our workplace culture if we couldn't even spark change in our own homes. Hence, the seed for this book was planted.

I was tired of hearing myself complaining and asking questions for which I had no answers. I was tired of reading about the challenges, the inequities, the bitching, and wanted to do something about it. What follows is a blueprint for enacting change, a plan to help you create strong partnerships, enhance loving relationships, affirm the structure of the family, and allow men and women to intentionally and consciously participate equally in their roles as parents.

In exploring parenting roles, I have interviewed almost 100 mothers and fathers, and I have heard the wide range of stories. Women who claim fulfillment, yet feel empty inside. Men who feel they can never please their wives. Women who are angry and resentful and resigned. Men who feel that the pressure to be successful doesn't leave them room to make choices based on their families. Women who do it all, and men who do little. Men who do it all, and women who do little. I've heard women's voices shake with emotion as they revealed their unhappiness, yet watched others glowing with the love of a supportive, adoring partner and children. Men have gotten very nervous, afraid that I will ask them a question that they don't know how to answer; others have listened attentively, relieved and eager to express their desire to parent. This book hopes to explore the deep, dark lake of our emotions—the psychic collage of our childhood and the experiences we lived through—and connect us with intention and action.

While I was conducting interviews for the book, women repeatedly asked, "When does this book come out? I need it!" My answer was always, "So do I! That's why I'm writing it!" In the beginning, I had to overcome resistance, not just from others, but from my own suspicious inner voice: This can't possibly work! Maybe this means I'm a bad mother, because I want to formally share parenting roles with my husband. I questioned my intentions—was I selfish, detached from my children, radical, or denying my biological destiny?

When in doubt, connect with the heart—and my heart told me that letting my husband into the lives of our children was the greatest gift I could give the kids, my husband, and our marriage. This seemingly simple act set in motion changes for our family that were nothing short of revolutionary.

Little did I know that as I began to write this book, I was rewriting our family life. We had the intention to change our parenting arrangement but no real idea how to do so. Remarkably—through heart-to-heart discussions and soul-searching, goal-setting, and negotiations with each other—the scales have tipped the other way. I now work in a full-time job outside of the home, and Gill works at home part-time. He is the primary parent, carpooling, managing the morning routine, child care, and school, with one foot in the work world. As for me, I am working full-time and have relinquished my primary parent status, yet I have a job that allows me to work a forty-hour week and still spend time with my children. We have scaled back our life. We have made a few unconventional choices and taken risks. By trading parenting roles, we have moments of deep understanding and raucous laughter. Just the other morning Gill, who now calls himself the Kitchen Bitch, told me he had shared his Beef Teriyaki recipe with a group of women at school. "What is happening to me? I'm chatting about recipes with the ladies?" he asked me wide-eyed and concerned—and then flexed his bicep to show me he was still the man of the house. Laughing at my sexy husband in his mock-macho pose, I grabbed my briefcase, kissed the kids, and ran out the door.

Just Kiss Me and Tell Me You Did the Laundry

CHAPTER 1

Intentional Parenting and Equality

"Marriage is not merely sharing the fettuccini,
but sharing the burden of finding the fettuccini
restaurant in the first place."

–Calvin Trillin

I was driving to work while listening to a national radio news show airing a special report on stay-at-home fathers. There were fathers being interviewed from a park. Fathers feeding and disciplining their children. Fathers reporting that they had no free time anymore. Fathers discussing the loneliness, wrestling with their identities, while their wives or partners worked all day away from home. Yet all of the fathers interviewed relished the time they were sharing with their children. They loved seeing them become "little people," growing close to them, and felt the emotional rewards were infinite. And that was the end of the story.

Was this really a news story? I thought. Men parenting and taking their kids to the park? If this was the criteria for breaking news, the phenomena of grandparents indulging their grandchildren and children pooping in pools must certainly be next. Stay-at-home fathering struck me as a nonstory. Wasn't the idea of women and men working together to raise their children commonplace enough not to be the exception to the rule? Then I realized that the point of the story was newsworthy simply as an updated version on the classic story of parenting. Like a remake of a classic movie where the plot remains the same, but the actors have changed: Parenting will always be hard, will often result in blows to confidence and waylaid careers and paychecks, and it is monotonous and even boring. The loving part is still easy for mothers *and* fathers, but the rest of it—the shopping, the meals, the disciplining, the requirement of parents to maintain consistency, the eye-rolling, the battles—that's the hard stuff. The simple truth beyond the day-to-day routine of it all is that the emotional rewards of loving our children are infinite. For both parents. Parenting is not something to be divided along gender lines, nor is it about socialized behaviors, cultural expectations, or guilt or "should haves." Parenting is a partnership of the highest calling and one that we must embark on with intention and love—together.

So now imagine this story on the radio: It starts with a couple in love, and a baby comes into their lives. In the night, when the baby wakes, they both jump out of bed at the same time; they are both comfortable holding, swaddling, and cooing to the baby; and their hearts burst wide open with the love they feel. They take turns taking the baby to the doctor, sorting through clothes as the child outgrows them, and planning outings with other new parents. The parents maintain their work lives yet alter jobs, when necessary and possible, to raise the child. As the child grows, the couple plans nutritious meals together, negotiates child care and housework, and together makes decisions about finances and career. The child is a member of an active and warm family, not the center of the family. The parents take time out from parenting to focus on their relationship, romance and shared activities, talking and laughing.

Farfetched? Maybe. Maybe not. Every change starts with a vision not of what is, but of what could be.

Rate Your Parenting Intentions

1. Would you refer to your relationship as an equal partnership?
2. Do you feel that you have equal decision-making influence?
3. Do you find yourself conceding in areas in which you're not comfortable?
4. Do you each have similar amounts of personal freedom?
5. Do you feel romantic love and connection with your partner?
6. Are there areas where you feel misunderstood, resentful, or underappreciated in your relationship?
7. Do you feel that your career goals are valued? Is earning power the main factor in assigning professional importance?
8. Are you equally sharing responsibility for, and knowledge of, your family's finances?
9. If there is a stay-at-home parent in your family, have you taken measures to financially protect this parent?
10. Do you value parenting as the most important priority for each of you?
11. Do you find yourself frustrated over who does housework and chores? Do you complain to others about this aspect of your life?
12. How do you nurture family life in your home?
13. Do you feel valued for your role in the family, as parent or breadwinner, or both?

Definitions for Understanding

Equal parenting means that both parents share in the responsibility of care for their children—from child care to child-related tasks. It means they intentionally choose parenting roles through mutual agreement and thoughtful discussion based on the tenets of equality. Whether or not parents fall under the label of a stay-at-home parent/breadwinner couple or dual-earner couple, they equally share in finding solutions for the care and well-being of the children.

PARENTING TOGETHER IS ALL ABOUT EQUAL PARENTING

"We are still suffering from the idea that children need one mother, in one home, twenty-four hours a day; that fathers are shadowy figures in a child's life; and that the child is a blank slate on which the parents write the script that is forever indelible."

—**Rosalind Barnett and Caryl Rivers**
in *She Works/He Works*

More and more, we hear stories of fathers staying home to care for children, or men working from home part-time in order to coparent. As a friend, Dennis, told me, "When I tell people that I stay home with my son 2 days a week, I still get an 'oh, that's so cute,' response." But men as primary parents, or formally involved in child care, are still a small minority. Mothers, we know, are the ones who change their lives to accommodate children. But today, with most couples working, equal parenting—where we share the care of the children—is a necessary reality. What is equal parenting? Equal parenting asks you to be your best self and to dedicate yourself to having a marriage based on equality, so that you may have the opportunity of sharing in the care of your precious children and home.

"What's wrong with the way things are?" Mothers get nervous that equal parenting means they're being asked to give up their bond with their children—that they will lose their favored-parent status. Some mothers are afraid to expect equal parenting, because they're afraid of what asking for it implies. We believe that if we want and ask our partners to formally contribute, we're somehow not "good mothers."

Fathers get scared and defensive, worried that they will have to sacrifice their work lives, ambition, and paychecks and put on an apron. They feel unacknowledged for their leap in parenting participation as compared with their own fathers and often feel trapped in their roles.

Once we release stereotypes and get past our fears, there seems to be little downside to equal parenting. Marriages are happier. Children grow up bonded to both parents. Mothers are stronger. And as equal parenting–based families trickle out into our communities, they influence the workplace and public policy.

Creating an Equal Parenting Agreement for YOUR Situation

In the chapters that follow, you will find ways to identify and discuss the specific obstacles to equal parenting in your own home. You'll be guided step-by-step with ideas to spark your own thinking as well as conversation starters to use to negotiate and amicably alter the structural issues that govern your family life. The ultimate goal of this book is to help you design and intentionally create parenting roles based on the ideal of equal parenting, so that your hopes and goals for your family match your intentions. As you work toward creating an Equal Parenting Agreement (EPA) with your spouse, keep in mind the following:

❋ Equal parenting is not necessarily defined as a 50/50 division of labor, with couples keeping scorecards.

❋ This is an evolving agreement that will change in response to job status, stages in your children's development, and your own changes of heart.

❋ There are many outside resources to help mediate.

❋ Change is always difficult; the process of equal parenting may be a long, but ultimately a deeply fulfilling, road for you and your partner.

❋ There is no downside. The benefits to equal parenting are tremendous, for our children, our relationships, and our communities.

❋ Remember to enjoy the process! If it feels like work, you may not be approaching it with the right frame of mind. This is especially important if your spouse seems reluctant—the lighter and more enjoyable you can keep the discussions, the more likely he'll stay engaged and work with you toward lasting change.

Each of the following chapters addresses the different areas that make up our lives—self, relationship, careers, children, and home. A series of exercises, steps, and negotiation points leads you to solutions that will work for your particular family dynamic. For example, the Loving Each Other chapter focuses on keeping your relationship strong, loving and open before, during, and after children. The chapter on Taking Care of Home and Hearth includes practical ways to create household standards, goals, and a comprehensive list of negotiation points. The elements in each chapter are:

Questions to help you and your partner explore beliefs, feelings, and histories

Exercises, including written or interactive ideas, for understanding each other, goal-setting, and establishing expectations

An Equal Parenting Love Story

Clara and Rich had a gorgeous little baby girl, Emily, after years of trying to conceive. At first, Clara, a nurse who found great meaning and purpose in her work with terminally ill patients, took time off from her job to stay at home. After 6 months, Clara returned to work, where she had negotiated a 4-day workweek. "I had mixed feelings about leaving Emily during the week," she explains, "but then my husband Rich decided to take 3 months off to full-time parent, so I felt great about it." Rich's employer supported his decision, although he wasn't paid during his time off.

Clara reported, "Rich embraced his role as a stay-at-home dad and completely loved it." At the same time, Clara realized that 4 days at the hospital was too much for her and switched to 3 days: "Maybe with certain jobs, a 4-day schedule is reasonable, but with nursing, my shifts constantly ran over—you cannot walk away from a patient because of the time clock." A much-changed Rich explains, "The time I spent seeing Emily grow made me realize how quickly it would go by—and I didn't want to miss it." As a result, Rich negotiated a 30-hour workweek. He was also able to work from home, eliminating his commute and allowing him to be available for emergencies or sick days. Their story ends with Emily in kindergarten. Five years of working part-time schedules had entailed major budget cutting. "We haven't gone on a vacation since the late 1990s!" Clara exclaims. Now, though, they both are working almost full-time hours again. They are proud of the choices they have made, and they are true partners in the care of Emily. "Not everyone has the flexibility with employers to do what we did, but it's so worth it to try and make it work."

Negotiation Points that allow you to assign responsibility for a list of parenting and household tasks and relationship and financial issues.

A Husband's Viewpoint are sidebars throughout the book, written by my husband, Gill, to provide a much-needed male perspective.

In a perfect world, you would have plenty of time to work through every exercise, negotiate every point, and contemplate all the words in this book. But the truth is, if you're reading this book, you're probably already a parent, and you know that the concept of "plenty of time" ended in the delivery room. So, use this book in whatever way works best for you—jump to chapters that apply to the areas where you're having difficulty; turn to the exercises and have at them with your mate; find the "Quick Tips" sidebars that identify the critical parts of each chapter; or flip straight to the negotiation points at the end of each chapter. However you choose to do the work, moving toward equal parenting will create a balance for yourself, your children, and your marriage.

WHY DID I WRITE THIS BOOK FOR WOMEN?

"You start in the home where things have not changed that much. There is still 'women's work.' And until that whole notion disappears, until child care and the drudge work are shared equally by men, all else is secondary. . . . We're not sitting around and talking about whether men can combine work and family."

—Jacqueline Jones, Brandeis University history professor and author of *American Work*

Change generally comes about spurred on by those who need it most, which is why I initially wrote this book for women. I recognize the irony of addressing only one half of the traditional parenting unit and realize it goes against the argument for the equal nature of responsibility. But I also believe that, in most cases, at this point in time, women will be the instigators of the discussion about parenting roles with their partners. (I'd be very happy to be proven wrong on this

Are You Kidding Me? The Shortcuts to Using This Book

Most parents have little to no time to spend designing their parenting roles— yet the time you spend working through the day-to-day issues, repairing present grievances, or stating parenting intentions is an investment in the brighter future of your family life.

If you feel that it's impossible to read this book in order, here are some tips on how to use it to get the most out of it when pressed for time.

- Go directly to the chapter that covers the "hot spots" of your marriage, such as housework imbalances, career trade-offs, or relationship sore spots.
- Take the quiz at the beginning of each chapter to help you identify your problem areas, and go to the corresponding sections.
- Go to the back of each chapter and look at the "Negotiation Points" section to identify tasks that need to be discussed.
- Go to the "Quick Tips" section in each chapter for immediate relief, knowing you need to focus on preventive health in the future.
- Leave the book in the bathroom for your partner while you boycott grocery shopping and spend an hour doing something self-affirming.

point!) The fact remains that women are the main readers of books on relationships and parenting. Overwhelmingly so. And it also remains true that in the majority of two-parent couples, women are the primary parent. If you're a man who has picked up this book in search of a more equal and intentional role in your family, you'll still find it useful. In the end, we're all in this together, and whether you are a nontraditional couple or a traditional couple, the book will have relevance to your situation.

FIVE REASONS WHY TODAY'S COUPLES NEED EQUAL PARENTING AGREEMENTS

Reason #1: The more equality we have in our marriages, the happier we are being married. Many years ago, while I was waiting for a bus, I saw a woman being threatened by a man. He was her boyfriend, or maybe her husband—and he was yelling at her and looking as if he might hit her. My adrenalin started pumping, and I intervened without thinking, quickly realizing two things: This man was huge (I was not), and the woman didn't want my help. In fact, she wanted everyone at the bus stop, including me, to ignore them. But I couldn't keep my mouth shut, and I got between the two to offer what I hoped was help for this woman. Luckily for me, another man, also huge, stepped alongside me, his presence quelling the situation.

Inequality and abuse of power is sometimes obvious, like at the bus stop. Other times, especially in our marriages, an imbalance of power is subtle. It's easy to ignore subtle power struggles, and an imbalance eventually becomes the accepted norm. One person may control financial decisions; another has no personal time or freedom to fulfill needs or goals. Some people lord sexual power over another by withholding intimacy. Maybe educational or career goals aren't valued equally. Perhaps the breadwinner is only valued for the money they make, or maybe the other person's role isn't considered important, because they make less or no money. As one stay-at-home mother of two quietly asked, "Do you know how I can convince my husband that what I do counts and is worth something?" When such a power imbalance exists in a relationship, it can be difficult to express emotions, such as anger or frustration—or to ask for more help or support.

When there is equality—when we have mutual respect and love for each other's role within the family—we are happier. When we share power in the critical areas that make up a family—home, work, emotional life, and parenting—we are more likely to succeed in having a great family life. A commitment to equality often means a better sex life. We divorce less. Our children thrive.

So here I am offering an intervention, not at the bus stop this time, but through this book in your hands. It's an offer of encouragement, for me and my husband and all couples, to be conscious when assessing our roles within our family—with equality and its reward of deep fulfillment as a baseline.

Reason #2: Equal parenting is a great message for children. Sociologists Scott Coltrane and Michele Adams of the University of California at Riverside found that children who participated in housework with their fathers had more friends; got along better with peers; and were less likely to be depressed, withdrawn, or cause trouble at school. As parents, we hope to teach our children how to cook, clean, make decisions, and set goals to prepare them with life skills—and the more both parents share in this, the better for the child. "When men perform domestic service for others, it teaches children cooperation and democratic family values," says Professor Coltrane. This paves the way for gender equity in their future relationships.

Beyond housework, intentional parenting teaches our children about negotiation, equality, and respect. When we negotiate our roles, we are modeling for our children that we respect each person's contribution to the family. It shows our children that their care is important enough for both parents to consider a worthy undertaking. Love is a verb, as they say, and performing the work of love, from grocery shopping to washing dishes, from reading *Pat the Bunny* to helping with homework, is the most powerful message you can give.

Reason #3: Equal parenting helps us meaningfully prioritize our lives. I had asked Glen if I could interview him after seeing him comfortably interacting with the kids at a school fundraiser. A father of two and a former executive, he amusingly described his life now as consulting 30 hours a week and spending the rest of the time "overly involved" in his children's school and sports activities.

But it wasn't always so, he explains, "When my wife sat me down and told me that it was time for us to strategize how we wanted to parent our children—*together*—I was taken aback at first. I felt a little angry, a little 'how dare you emasculate me,' but it was clear that until that point—and our children were, I think, about five and seven then—my wife had made all of the sacrifices and changes to her life and her career, and I had just kind of coasted. I showed up at the end of my workday and saw the kids for an hour—if I wasn't working late, and I usually was. I lived for the weekends. But my wife was asking me to coparent, and she was asking me to prioritize what was important to us—and even though it was difficult, it was also easy: My family was vastly more important to me than my work. My paycheck fulfilled me, and it was hard to let go of the stature I had at work, but it was only a superficial satisfaction. I wanted to be with my children and have a terrific marriage—not exclusive to doing good paid work—but it was more important than working 50- or 60-hour weeks and having a corner office, so to speak. My wife pointed out that she would share the financial responsibility, and we would be partners in contributing to the family income, just as we would be partners in caring for the children. I married my wife because she was smart and strong, and I certainly couldn't argue with her logic—or with the amazing opportunity it presented us all."

Reason #4: Equal parenting supports both parents in having a rich family life and a rewarding exterior life. In the first years of my daughter's life, I worked from home part-time and my husband Gill worked long hours, commuted, and would sometimes go days without seeing her before she went to bed at night. When the weekend came, he just wanted to be home, cuddle and interact with her, and curl up on the couch with me for a movie and comfort food. Gill would re-enter his emotional life; his workweek was done, he had left the exterior world of commuter trains and office demands, and he wanted to inhabit his interior self, his heart. I was the complete opposite. I'd been home most of the week with Ella and just wanted to get out of the house. It was almost like we were "serial parenting" where I was "on" during the week, then turned off when he took over on the weekend.

While Gill craved family time, I craved an exterior life of interacting with others and feeling the stimulation of sights and sound beyond the playground. It was apparent to us that our parenting roles were out of whack. We both felt that we were missing out on some part of our own lives—and instead of writing it off as typical or "this is the reality of parenting" we were committed to finding work and family balance for both of us. We had no idea how to do this, but we hoped that if we began to keep our intention of equal parenting in mind, that we might get there. Equal parenting asks that you each:

❋ Take care of your emotional needs and growth.
❋ Commit to the work of making a healthy, loving, respectful marriage.
❋ Devote yourself to your children, their well-being, and their care.
❋ Value each other's goals; share in goal- and decision-making.
❋ Share the responsibility of house-related chores.

Reason #5: Equal parenting is good for society. It's scary to change traditional mores. But tradition for tradition's sake isn't necessarily good. There is tradition worth holding onto and tradition worth letting go. Remember, for women, not having voting or property rights was a tradition. Racism and war are traditions. And there is the traditional 1950s model for a wife, demystified by cultural historian Marilyn Yalom in *A History of the Wife*, "In real life many housewives resented the monotony, drudgery, and isolation of their daily lives. All the consumer products intended to make their work easier and their lives more pleasant (according to the marketing mavens of the day), all the newly fabricated mood pills like Dexedrine prescribed by indulgent doctors, all the talk of woman's biological destiny and sacred place in the family could not hide the sense of frustration and alienation that some wives were feeling in their suburban cages."

There is no doubt that traditional roles have changed dramatically since the 1950s, as women have entered the workforce in droves, and the number of dual-earner parents far exceeds the number of stay-at-

A Husband's Viewpoint

No Guts, No Glory

It's time for a sports analogy: no pain, no gain. But this kind of pain is new to us. We have not been socially conditioned to make sacrifices around career—or even personal time—to affect a balanced parenting situation. Many of us, including myself, grew up conditioned as the hunter, to go out and be the breadwinner, and in this "traditional" way we would fulfill our parenting, relationship, and family responsibilities. If we were lucky, we'd be at the kid's game, or the school play, and certainly we'd be at the birthday party. Getting more involved tkaes new thinking. I remind myself, "Okay, I chose to be with these kids. If I continued to be out of the home 60 to 70 hours a week, I would miss so much of their development—and I am not going to let that happen."

Truth is, equal parenting takes guts and self-confidence: You have to know the power of the emotional payoff and every time you catch your kid's grin or get a huge hug when you otherwise would have been scrapping for clams, you are reminded of your subtle, but very powerful victory—the one where the kids and parents both win.

A spot of advice for spouses: Realize that it doesn't happen overnight, and be sensitive to the vulnerabilities many men will experience in making this great shift, this leap.

home/breadwinner parents. Still, women are largely the primary parents, whether they work full-time for pay or raise children full-time. Men are becoming more involved with child-raising and housework than ever before, but there's still a discrepancy in most relationships— often laughed off by couples, "You know men, they just can't clean like we can," or "She's just better with the kids, so she gets up at night." But it's not funny.

When it comes to marriage, it's easier to believe that men are from Mars and women from Venus, because it doesn't require us to change, to ask our mates to change, or to do the work needed to make our relationships better. Asking for and risking change means risking failure—and that can be terrifying. But what if we ask, and they say yes? What if we insist? As told in their book, *She Works/He Works*, Rosalind Barnett and Caryl Rivers found that fathers are not interested in going back to the traditional sole breadwinner role and are more interested in finding new ways to parent. They don't find this threatening to their manhood in the least: "Most would laugh if you called them weak or genderless. In fact, they find that their involvement adds richness and meaning to their lives. They may be buying into more stress and juggling than their fathers ever did, but the rewards of their lives generally outweigh the problems. They are increasingly willing to sacrifice on-the-job advancement for time with their children."

When men are formally involved in parenting, families will benefit—but all society will reap the rewards. As men become engaged parents, they will be our partners in changing public policy and the workplace environment. They'll fight for real dollars for their schools and parks. They will understand the need for quality child care for all families. They will be shocked at the low wages paid to teachers and care providers. They will want to find viable solutions to financially protect stay-at-home parents. They will realize the importance of paid parental leave. They might consider the welfare of children throughout the world from an entirely new perspective.

Can you imagine what we can do with their help?

HOW DO I BEGIN TO TAKE INTENTIONAL STEPS TOWARD EQUAL PARENTING?

"And yet the responsibility for inequality falls squarely on our own shoulders: when we function discontentedly in a capacity that we accepted without question, doing nothing to correct the situation, we're imposing inequality on ourselves. As has been so wisely remarked, 'No one can take our power away; we've got to give it away.'"

—Maurice Taylor and Seana McGee,
The New Couple

It's a nice idea, doing all our parenting with conscious intent, but in practice, how can we possibly achieve this type of shared responsibility? It's not about drawing a line in the laundry, so to speak. It's about being committed to the tenets of a marriage based on equal responsibility for parenting. A few years ago, researchers at the Colorado State University Department of Human Development and Family Studies conducted a study interviewing 47 middle-class, dual-earner couples with children. Based on their study results, the foundation principles of successful dual-earner marriages are adapted and presented below.

Strive to be a whole person. When we don't love ourselves, it's hard to have the inner fiber to generously love those around us. Loving ourselves means taking care of all the layers that make up a person— emotional, physical, spiritual, and intellectual—as best we can. We strengthen our emotional self by honoring our feelings, working on our personal growth, and overcoming emotional blocks and obstacles. We take care of our physical self by paying attention to what our body needs and participating in healthy behaviors and activities. Our spiritual self is nurtured through exploring or finding a practice that keeps us grounded, gives us perspective, and helps us recognize—and be part of—the larger community around us. Our intellectual self is stimulated through learning, achieving our goals, and challenging ourselves though hobbies and external interests. Attending to all facets of our self allows us to be a strong, complete parent and person.

Commit to a healthy, respectful, loving marriage—and to doing the work to make it so. A happy marriage bequeaths a happy home which bequeaths happy children. Your marriage is the foundation of your family, good or bad. A strong marriage provides support and structure where children and adults can flourish. An equal marriage partnership constitutes shared decision-making around finances, child care, career, and home. It means having equal influence in the decision-making process—and being equally responsible for finding solutions to the daily and long-term situations that arise in life. A healthy marriage is one where communication, honesty, and emotional maturity are the norm. When you're "out of whack," it means finding ways to regain your balance, through outside help or resources and taking the time to make it right. Marriage takes work, and committing to a good marriage means you must do the "work of love," as feminist and author bell hooks calls it, to create a great marriage.

Value working life and goals equally. Equal parenting gives both parents the opportunity to alter their working lives to be with their children. When two people become parents it often makes sense for one or both to downsize a career. But when designing equal parenting roles, you must agree that your careers and goals be of equal value, even if they're not financially equal. If one spouse has a low-paying job at a nonprofit, and the other is a highly paid computer engineer, it may be a financial necessity to evaluate your roles taking income earning potential into account. You may want to consider other options, such as foregoing the new car, the pool membership, or dressing your children in designer clothing. Ask each other these questions and be open to continual discussion as you take the first steps in exploring your options. For most families, there are no easy answers. We want to be present for our children, yet we live in a society that demands long working hours. We are afraid of stepping off a career track, losing earning power and professional momentum. Equal parenting ensures that neither one's dreams and goals are unwillingly sacrificed.

Share the responsibility of parenting, including child care and child-related tasks. Historically, traditional couples appeared to compartmentalize their life: The kitchen was the wife's domain, and the garage was the man's; the children were hers, and a paid job was his. This division undermined both men and women, blocking men from openly participating in their children's lives and blocking women from careers and the outside world. Today, the company man could just as easily be the company woman, and stay-at-home fathers—while still newsworthy—brag about their kitchen prowess.

Caring for our children together is a joy. Imagine both parents knowing the homeopathic remedy that works best for their three-year-old or being able to cover at a teacher conference, PTA meeting, or music class, because both are fully involved in and knowledgeable about what's going on in their child's life.

Share responsibility for housework and family sustenance. My daughter and I were picking herbs from the garden after my workday recently (and my son was eating red peppers, but that's another story). "What should we do with these herbs?" I asked. Ella knew: "We should give them to daddy, because he's the cooker." I laughed out loud—but then, curious, asked, "Am I the cooker too?" She nodded, remembering the time when I was the main cooker, "But he's the cooker now." This was a watershed moment, and as I later recounted the story to Gill, he too thought it was noteworthy and amusing. "Is it hard for you?" He asked. I was surprised to admit that it is sometimes painful. Why I need to be thought of as the cooker, the laundry lady, or the housie (our word for the houseparent) beats me, but I try to notice my feelings and where they come from—an ingrained belief that good mothers keep a good house, for example—and let the critical voice go.

An active family life and home life is an essential component of a healthy family. From the food you eat and holidays you celebrate to housekeeping and car maintenance, sharing the responsibility says that you respect your partner enough to not assume that the other will pick up after you or take care of you.

The Gender Politics of It All

Examining gender politics in your household, what rings true for your marriage?

1. Men are generally in positions of power in society—but this can also keep them trapped.
2. Women are disempowered because of financial dependence, which can limit their assertion of rights, equality, and selves.
3. A vicious marital cycle begins when a wife pressures a detached or emotionally unavailable husband for more conversation and help; the husband resists, and the wife pushes more.
4. Men still earn higher wages than women in general.

QUESTIONS TO ASK YOURSELF

I grew up in a traditional family, with a mom who stayed home and a dad who worked a lot and went on business trips. Held up against the standards of her day, my mother was an excellent stay-at-home mother. We had an enormous vegetable garden, she cooked delicious meals, headed my Girl Scout troop, and ebulliently read and sang to us (and my mother is indeed ebullient!).

My parents were good at parenting, but not good at being married to each other. They divorced as I was entering my teens. My brother and I lived with my father, who worked full-time and took care of us—making our meals, providing a stable home environment, and trying his best to monitor us so that we didn't get into trouble. He was the original soccer mom—before the minivan—with an oversized big blue van, a respectable maxivan, if you will. On many Saturdays he drove anywhere from five to ten 13-year-old girls to soccer matches. At that time, it was unusual for a father to have sole custody of his children, an opinion often voiced by the mothers in our town in a disapproving yet impressed way. Our idea of family culture was eating tacos, followed by a big bowl of popcorn, while watching Star Trek together. My father combined his work as an insurance executive with raising two teenagers using lists, humor, a housecleaner, and an occasional scare tactic as his parenting backup. He managed exceedingly well, and I learned, first-hand, that both parents could parent, and that I needed them both.

As a side benefit of this unconventional parenting arrangement, I developed a knack for challenging the traditional gender roles. A life-time of asking questions brought out some critical issues that I believe remain at the heart of whether intentional, equal parenting roles can be negotiated among spouses:

❋ Can women give up the idea of "being taken care of" financially?

❋ Can women consider themselves equal financial partners?

❋ Can men let go of the idea of having a wife to buttress their career and family? Can men consider themselves equally responsible for raising children?

❋ How do we redefine our gender roles as multifaceted instead of one-dimensional: homemakers or breadwinners, nurturers or he-men?

A CHALLENGE FOR YOU, THE READER

The Equal Parenting Agreement challenges women to stand up in their relationships and not fall into traditional gender roles by default, at the expense of yourselves. It's difficult for most women to stand up to our mates when we've been told "don't rock the boat" and trained to be pleasers. Just as we changed the makeup of corporate America and the workplace for the better, it's now time for women to redefine motherhood and family for the benefit of all. As Marilyn Yalom has observed, "Americans are not giving up on wifehood. Instead, they are straining to create more perfect unions on the basis of their new status as coearners and their husbands' fledgling status as cohome-makers. I suspect that the death of the 'little woman' will not be grieved by the multitude, even if society must endure severe birth pangs in producing the new wife."

The Equal Parenting Agreement challenges men to formally as-sume more parenting and household responsibility. Men are being de-prived of the opportunity to participate in the lives of their children and run the household—and they risk missing out on the emotional richness that these roles offer. With partners sharing financial responsibility, the pressure to single-handedly provide family financial comfort is alleviated, and men are able to pursue greater involvement in the arenas of raising children and maintaining a home and family life.

As my life and relationship has shifted into the realm of equal parenting, I see that it doesn't solve every problem, smooth over all marital insurgencies, or secure the fairy-tale-perfect life. We have discovered, though, a deeper understanding of each other and our realities: Gill knows the pediatrician better than I right now and gets frustrated with my overbearing presence in the kitchen during dinnertime, as I try to reclaim my former domain. I understand how hard it is to come home after a long workday and emotionally give of myself. I hear myself muttering, "Cut me some slack," and could swear that Gill used this exact expression when I would pressure him the minute he walked through the door after work. I see Gill making lists of school lunch ideas and adding them to the shopping list, and I have to hold myself back from bursting into "Glory, Glory, Hallelujah!" He is anxious to work, yet understands the challenge to his work schedule when a child is sick or during a school holiday—just as I used to— and we negotiate the rough spots. In a recent discussion of finances, he thanked me for being his financial partner, "I'm lucky I can count on you," and I thought, as I saw him going over the alphabet with our daughter, with our son on his lap, "We're all lucky."

CHAPTER 2

Strengthening Yourself

"Women do not have to sacrifice personhood if they are mothers. They do not have to sacrifice motherhood in order to be persons. Liberation was meant to expand women's opportunities, not to limit them."

—Elaine Heffner

Ten days after my first child was born, while still hopeful about hanging on to my former life, I had the notion of going out to dinner with my husband: My mother could watch the baby, and we would only be an hour or so. I showered, body still aching from 32 hours of labor, put on makeup, and wore a dress— a simple linen sheath that hid most of my body. Luckily, my engorged breasts protruded slightly more than my huge belly. We went to one of our favorite places, a hip, lively tapas bar close to our home. I looked around and smiled and thought, "Our lives are exactly the same as before." As we walked up to the bar, I noticed several men checking me out. This, I thought, is how it feels to have large breasts. "I'm not looking so bad," I chuckled to myself. Gazing down to admire my new breasts, horror struck. My milk had let down, and I had two wet spots the size of silver dollar pancakes on my dress. I grabbed my husband,

The Self-Analysis Quiz

Parenting can mean that our identities fall into a black hole. Answering the questions below will help you determine what parts of your self may be headed for lost-in-space status.

1. Do you accidentally talk in the third person about yourself, such as "Mommy wants another glass of wine," to waiters in restaurants? Do you even go to restaurants?

2. Name the last time you had no roots or gray, shaved legs, and a perfectly accessorized outfit at the same time, not counting your wedding.

3. Are you still wearing nursing bras even though your children are in braces? Is your most recent pair of sexy underwear as threadbare as tissue?

4. Speaking of sexy, what is the sexiest thing about you? What makes you feel sexy?

5. Do you feel connected with your body? What activities help you feel stronger and more physically capable?

pointing out the geyser spill, and we burst out laughing. I got it. My life, my body, my heart, my marriage would never be the same again.

My public letdown was the perfect introduction to motherhood. I thought I was above the issues of normal mothers. I thought my emotional life would remain the same as before. I was certain that my parenting would be different and that my children wouldn't be obsessed with Disney movies or have a Barbie collection to rival collectors on eBay. And I knew that, without a doubt, I would have an equal parenting arrangement with my devoted and loving partner. After all, these were our children, and we were in harmony about both parenting and our careers. What could possibly go wrong?

6. Name three activities you'd like to do on the weekend, alone. When was the last time you had a weekend getaway alone or with friends?

7. What were the last two books you read? The last magazine article that you spoke with a friend about? The political issue that motivated you to send an e-mail to your senator?

8. If you could start a club, what would be the purpose, and whom would you invite?

9. If you could work on any emotional or psychological issues, what would they be?

10. When was the last time you had a personal goal that you achieved?

11. How much time do you spend feeling guilty? Resentful? Angry? Complaining? Fearful?

12. How much time do you spend feeling blessed and grateful? Peaceful? Confident and trusting? Generous?

If I have learned anything in these last 5 years of mothering, it is that it's an unpredictable journey. My emotions have boomeranged from amusement and joy to anger and resentment. For the moment, I have settled into intense love and peaceful acceptance. My relationship with my husband has been on a parallel journey: We've gone from being new parents, to couples counseling, to a partnership that usually works—punctuated with feelings ranging from admiration to jealousy. We have settled into deep respect, tenderness, occasional bursts of stressed-out anger, and a "light at the end of the tunnel" attitude. Sometimes it feels the past 5 years have whizzed by—our first child is off to kindergarten, and she's long-limbed, thoughtful, and in-

Quick Tips

If you are in need of urgent care, here are four things in this chapter that might have the most immediate impact:

1. Plan an activity, ritual, or event that is all about you, taking care of yourself, and loving yourself. Gym and sauna. Trip to the bookstore. A day in nature. Yoga retreat.

2. Your affirmation for the week: *Feeling guilty serves no purpose; I'm doing the best I can to love my children, my partner, and especially myself.* Breathe deeply.

3. Read the section, "Get Rid of Your Mother Martyr" on page 44.

4. After the kids have gone to bed, don't clean or watch mindless TV: Do "The Goals and Dreams Interview" exercise on page 53. Let your imagination go wild.

dependent. Yet, when I'm up with my infant son from 1:00 A.M. to 6:00 A.M., 5 years measured by middle of the night hours seems a very long time.

There is no denying the change children bring about in our lives. But this upheaval need not be an excuse to neglect our own needs and development. Rather, it can provide us with a grand opportunity: a chance to recreate our relationship with our partners. We can choose to nurture our children together, in a relationship based on equality: equality around decision-making; equally sharing responsibility and accountability; and equally valuing the needs and goals of each and the roles we inhabit.

This chapter focuses on how to strengthen yourself and embrace all the possibilities inherent in motherhood—to be your best self, to fortify your marriage, and to give and experience love in its fullest, most complex, most sacred state.

BECOMING A MOTHER

"Women are said to be naturally inclined to motherhood, to bonding with their babies, to nurturance, patience, and generosity. Real mothers know that mothering is not a reflexive behavior but an acquired art."

—Natalie Angier, *Woman*

From the moment you become a mother, you join a powerful club of women. Like mother bears, we fight mightily for our cubs. We begin by cherishing their peach fuzz and tininess, and as they grow, we admire their emerging little selves, through tantrums, first days of school, and the fits and starts of daily life. It is an awesome experience to learn firsthand about a mother's love for her child.

As Andrea, a career coach, described her first year with her daughter, "We were both blindsided and blinded by the love of our child," she said. This newfound love doesn't mean that we don't crack at 3:00 A.M., lose our temper over senseless irritations, or sit our kids in front of the television so that we can have a break, check e-mail, or sneak a bowl of ice cream we don't feel like sharing. Instead, this overwhelming love enables us to be the best person we can be for our children. And it's a relief to know that, most of the time, we come through: We can stay up half the night; we can weather children who reject us for periods of time; we can give selflessly and do things that previously seemed impossible. It feels easy and natural in light of the intensity of our love for our children.

It is this same love that often blinds us. We can become so caught up in the needs of others that we forget who we were—the essence of what makes us unique—and come to believe it's no longer important. We backburner our relationships and spouses, convincing ourselves there will be other years to reconnect. We let go of our goals, dreams, and hopes for ourselves, putting them into our children, and one day wake up feeling empty and lonely. We compromise, again and again, doing what we hope is best for our children and our family. As a mother of school-age children, a teacher, explained, "I love what motherhood has taught me and all the new facets of my personality that have emerged because of it. I miss things about myself, though, and it's not my old life I miss, as much as who I was. Sometimes my husband suggests that I take a day on the weekend away from the kids. It's a great offer, but the sad part is that I'm not even sure what to do, and I have these feelings that I'm undeserving of this personal time. What did I used to do on a free Saturday? I'm not sure how I got to this place and lost myself."

Many husbands echoed almost identical sentiments about their wives. A father of three and sales manager admits, "My wife is the most loving, amazing mother. But I miss her being my wife. For fear of sounding selfish or childish myself, I miss our relationship. I miss seeing her light up when we discussed something she loved, some passion, whether it was a work project, a friend, politics, anything. Now, she's lost some confidence or something—and this affects lots in our relationship, like our sex lives. I'm sure I've changed, too, but it doesn't feel as extreme."

It's perceptions like these that cause us to wring our hands in frustration as we hear our partners complain that we're "not the same" or "you never have time for me" or "what's the big deal?" when we feel like we are struggling to keep our balance, caught between the demands of two—or more—worlds.

For men the shift into fatherhood isn't as extreme. Becoming a father is more subtle and generally doesn't require life changes: the physical demands of pregnancy and nursing, the structural change of a maternity leave and part-time work, the mental shifts women make—some gladly, some not—to our careers and goals.

Popular books, such as *The Bitch in the House, Flux,* and *I Don't Know How She Does It,* are speaking for us with eloquence, humor, and occasionally fighting words, exploring the conflicting feelings and parenting roles in transition around us. What no one discusses, though, is the topic of making our spouses our parenting partners. Like the proverbial elephant in the corner, the issue is as ignored in our conversations with girlfriends as it is in the general consciousness of the country when discussing child care, parenting, and work and family balance. Whether studying the effect of putting our children in extensive day care or examining the relationship between mothers and nannies, the elephant screams out: What about the father? Where is he in the parenting equation? Why aren't women speaking up—demanding—that the same questions and opportunities be put forth to their spouses?

Before we invite our spouses to accept equal parenting responsibility with us, we must begin with strengthening ourselves. As women adrift in a sea of confusion, overwhelming love, compromise, and longing, our anchor is easy to reclaim. It's the stone weight of our love for our family; the wish of equality for our sisters and daughters; the hope for equal parenting for our brothers and sons; and our wish for our partners to share in the emotional richness of parenthood.

Exploring Feelings about Motherhood

Basking in our mother role and all the joys and cuddles it entails is a wonderful thing, but it's just as important to understand our guilt and inner critic. I suggest that you journal your answers, but you might want to bring this up among friends, or just ponder a question for the day during your commute time. Pay attention to your feelings. There are no right answers.

- If you haven't yet had children, how do you expect to feel as a new mother? What are your hopes and fears?
- What was most unexpected about motherhood?
- What has been the most difficult time period for you since having children?
- What has been the most peaceful or playful time?
- Have you consciously or unconsciously made choices to parent based on your mother's model? How has motherhood changed you?
- How has your relationship with your parents changed?
- What are three pieces of advice you would give to new mothers?

HOW ARE WE STRUGGLING?

"After two decades in which boomers managed to make children the raison d'être not only of their lives but of the culture at large, another version of motherhood is beginning to seep out, with some mothers speaking up—in the impassioned tones of those breaking a taboo—about the drudgery of child care, the isolation of the playground and their loss of identity."

—**Elizabeth Hayt,** *The New York Times*

Many of us are afraid that if we question our feelings about motherhood or our roles as mothers, people will question our devotion to our children, so we keep quiet—"mum's the word." We wryly embrace the guilt and the power struggle with our partners, and we believe that tacit acceptance is our fate as mothers. In her book, *The Mask of Motherhood*, Susan Maushart says, "The mask of motherhood is what keeps women silent about what they feel and suspicious of what they know. It divides mother from daughter, sister from sister, friend from friend. It creates an abrupt and tragic chasm between adults who have children and adults who don't. . . . It pits male parents against female, amplifying the disjuncture between the verbs 'to mother' and 'to father.'" The silence and unresolved confusion take a heavy toll on our psyches and marriages, and on our children, who undoubtedly sense our discontent.

Stephanie, a mother of two teenagers and a full-time bank manager, explains her nightly routine: "I get home from my workday and immediately, I'm charging around my house obsessed with laundry and dinner with four food groups. My husband is able to relinquish this responsibility and worry to me, even though we both work full-time—and it pisses me off every single day! It's as if I have to remind him—we're *both* working here, buddy! There's definitely a wall between us, and neither of us are happy about it—but we don't know how to fix it. My boys will often escape to their rooms when the tension becomes unbearable." Underlying her relationship struggle is Stephanie's belief that she take on the entire responsibility of parenting, "I know I should stop doing everything and insist that he pay attention and take charge of more around the house. But for some reason, I stop short of asking and requiring that he do it, probably be-

A Husband's Viewpoint

When Mommy Becomes Daddy

Karen and I had been married for 2 years before our first child was born. As soon as we got home from the hospital (maybe even before), my wife changed. She heard every sound. She knew when Ella wasn't feeling well. Her every movement seemed to be driven by her instincts to protect our baby and keep our home safe and structured. In short, she turned into a mom.

I changed, too. I felt I went into a higher state of awareness, but it paled in comparison to Karen's mothering instinct. Because I wasn't biologically connected in the same way as Karen was, it seemed harder for me to feel the immediate closeness with our daughter. Whereas Karen had known for months, I was essentially meeting the baby for the first time at birth. Even for men who are emotionally sensitive and attuned, we need some time to get to know this new little person. But even though I may not have had the primal rush of child-rearing instinct that overcame my wife, as a new father, I still felt compelled to somehow help around the house, do what I

cause I hear my mother's irritating voice—'but *you're* the mother!'" Whether driven by guilt, social pressures, or her own internal voices, Stephanie feels primarily responsible for ensuring the health and safety of her children.

Fueling the idea that women are responsible for the welfare of the children is the "women can have it all" phenomenon. What this phenomenon should really be called is "women can DO it all." We can work outside of the home, take care of the children, and then also work inside of the home—all by ourselves. A bogus definition of equality if ever there was one. Naturally we fail, or could to remain sane, listen, and be responsive to the needs of the both Karen and Ella.

Karen was the primary parent, working part-time at home, for the first 4 years of our children's lives. Then we made a shift for Karen to work full-time. And I was shocked to see how easily my wife checked out and left it all to me. Just like that. Off to work she went. And it was no picnic! As I shifted to part-time work and full-time primary parenting, I suddenly developed a whole new set of senses. Now I'm the one who is most often the first to wake up at any peep in the night (formerly a truck rumbling through our bedroom wouldn't have woken me up). I'm most concerned about the quantity of food in the house and am now the stronger disciplinarian and rules enforcer.

It became clear to me that despite the biological distance I had from my kids, my parenting instincts can still kick in when they are called upon. And don't think the children don't appreciate my new sensitivity. In fact, now my kids accidentally call my wife "Daddy" quite frequently!

we feel like we're failing even if we're succeeding. We can never, ever do enough: We don't do as much at our jobs as we think we should; we would like to spend more quality time with our children; our house is never clean or nice enough; and surely our marriage could use a tune-up, at the very least. As we try to hold back the tide of life, creating endless to-do lists, hiring more help, and hustling around at the speed of light, our emotional strength weakens.

One of the biggest emotional tolls is a mother's self-confidence. For those women staying at home as full-time parents, self-esteem can fall for a variety of reasons, from losing the independence a paycheck brings to lack of mental stimulation and challenge. Those working outside of the home struggle with the challenge of work and family balance. And there is no quick fix to be found for either group of women. There's simply too much to do when you want to love and parent your children in the best way possible. Amazingly, many of us are afraid to look to our partners as equal problem-solvers in the equation. As Ruth Priest, self-described political activist and housewife, wrote in an opinion piece in the *San Jose Mercury News*, "When women of the '70s fought for access to careers, they never intended to warehouse their children. We thought that with the help of men we would develop new ways of parenting and running the house. We thought both parents could work part time, giving children more time with fathers. We changed our language from mothering to parenting, but little else actually changed."

The truth today is that men *are* doing more around the house and becoming more emotionally available fathers than ever before—and most men want to be more involved with their children. Change is occurring slowly, though. The idea that men and women are equally responsible for their children is still a strange concept to most. Like Stephanie, the majority of women are working outside of the home— and attempting to "do it all"—but for many, their efforts are built on a foundation of feelings of hopelessness and resentment. For the good of our families and society, we must move beyond guilt, complaints, and confusion and begin changing the storyline. For women, this chapter is a call to action. If we are strong and secure within ourselves, it becomes easier to work with our partners to create intentional parenting roles.

THE EQUAL PARENTING AGREEMENT TO STRENGTHEN YOURSELF

I commit to strengthening myself by loving and taking care of myself. I value myself and realize that my dreams, goals, and identity are not worth sacrificing.

While the EPA sections in other chapters focus on exploring and negotiating agreements with our partners, the goal of this EPA section is to ensure that you are first and foremost taking inventory of your own emotions and life as a mother or mother-to-be. It's a promise to commit to self-awareness and self-care—with a plan that will reel you in when you've cast your hopes, dreams, and needs out to sea.

Specifically, by strengthening yourself, you will be able to make healthier choices. You can parent from a place of integrity and love. You are better able to build an equal partnership with your mate. And you can show your children what it means to be a whole person—a whole person who is a mom and much more. Your first building block is self-love. Through self-love—giving yourself permission to take care of your emotional and physical needs—you will have the strength and purpose to create loving, equal parenting with your partner.

Before You Begin: Love Yourself First

One of the gifts of being a woman is that you can go anywhere, anytime and connect with other women who will listen to your story and share their own truth. On the bus, in the supermarket, at the park, at the cafeteria, women bond over universal experiences, and being a mother is one of the equalizers. Recently, I was on BART, the San Francisco Bay Area's version of the subway, and I began speaking with another woman who had a technology magazine in her lap but was busy filling out a form—an elementary school application, I later found out. She had noticed that I was reading an academic book on work and family balance and immediately wanted to talk: "I am so sick of this debate on women working," she said, "There really should be no debate. Like most women, I work. My life outside of my children is important to me. And this doesn't mean I love my children less. Just like men, I want to have a family and working life. The only reason there is a so-called debate is because we feel ridiculously guilty and responsible for everything. It should be much simpler than this."

This woman had it right, I thought. Our guilt and other negative emotions had undermined our most effective equal parenting negotiator: self-love. Most women have been taught to be pleasers or mediators, to take care of others, to smooth things over. Older generations of women have shown us, by example, the importance of supporting a husband's career and goals. Although it seems like feminism should have taught us to speak up, our old habits die hard. We're still learning how to make our presence count in boardrooms and bedrooms; we're still learning to love ourselves as much as we love our partners and children.

When we practice self-love, we believe our goals and dreams are as important as those of our mates. We hold our partners—and our relationships—to high expectations. We know the value of our time and parenting expertise. Self-love gives us the confidence to ask our spouses to be our true partners in life. When loving ourselves fully, we access an untapped reservoir of love to share with our children and spouse, friends and humanity.

How Can You Love Yourself?

For those of you who use affirmations to help keep your mind focused and energized on what's important in your life, here are some thoughts that can help you. Read through them and find the ones that you need to work on—then repeat them at some regular time in your day, such as when you're brushing your teeth or waiting at the bus stop.

- I forgive myself for not being perfect.
- I forgive myself for trying too hard to be.
- I reject the negative voices in my head. I am stronger than they are.
- I reject the negative voices of others. It's just background noise.
- I embrace the truth of my emotions: the good, the bad, and the ugly.
- I will rediscover who I am now. Woman and mother.
- I will rediscover my goals, my hopes, and my dreams.
- My goals are important. My hopes are important. My dreams are important. I will commit them to memory.
- I will build a support group of peers and enjoy their companionship.
- I will receive all the love and support that I need in my life.

The Ground Rules: We're All in This Together

Our choices around parenting—to stay at home, to work, to waffle—are never easy. Just because we've taken one path doesn't mean it's personally fulfilling, good for our children, or right for us. Our choices are never black and white. I have heard comments from women judging or feeling judged by other women about their choices: Sheila fumed over a new friend's announcement "I don't *have* to work," oblivious that work was a vital part of Sheila's life and unintentionally flashing financial privilege. Many women admitted to judging mothers who worked long workweeks and traveled, secretly and self-righteously thinking, "How can she possibly do that? I would *never* . . ."—while at the same time envying the business trips, career progression, and freedom.

Public opinion is as conflicted as women's. Opinion polls routinely find that people still believe it's better to have one parent, especially the mother, at home, citing parental inattention as a very serious problem in today's family. Conversely, though, 83 percent of us believe that women in the workplace are a change for the better, and two-thirds of parents say having one parent stay home is an unrealistic option in today's world.

Even when we make a choice that we know in our hearts is the right choice for our family, we continually have moments of self-doubt. Janet, mother of two, loves her full-time job as an office manager at a healthcare facility and contributes half of the family income. She has a wonderful nanny taking care of her youngest child, but when she comes home at the end of the day, she hears her son call the nanny "mommy." Janet explains that she knows she's fortunate to have such extraordinary child care, but she's devastated by this—and almost instantly the pain of leaving her children, like a raw nerve ending, sends out signals to all other negative thoughts: "I feel a horrible wave come over me about working, which includes feelings of guilt, shame, selfishness, and insecurity."

On the flipside, there is Donna, a stay-at-home mom who has given up her human resources job at a bank to be with her son, now a toddler. She adores her temporary hiatus as a housewife and mom, providing a beautiful, loving home environment for her husband and son. But after spending 2 hours at a company cocktail party with her husband, she has a crisis of confidence. Donna recounts, "I heard the emptiness of people's

Talking with Other Mothers

Talk with a close, trusted female friend who has chosen a different parenting path than you, and ask if you can openly discuss each other's decision-making process. Gently share your judgments, biases, or the secret envy you might have about each other's life. Discuss your perceptions. Do you think the other has it easier? Is she a more committed mother? How did your own mother's choice influence your decision making? Remember to acknowledge and respect how difficult parenting choices can be—and how sensitive we are to others' criticisms.

words telling me, 'It's so great that you are home with your kids. That's so important.' It's like I'm a Girl Scout, and they're buying my cookies just to be nice and make me go away.'" She feels boring and lackluster and believes she has little to contribute to any conversation.

As we travel on the road of parenting, we must honor and value the choices of our colleagues-in-mothering. As judgments surface— on yourself and others—stop the critical voice. Instead, focus on messages of support and compassion for all the challenges of mothering—and recognize that we are all doing the best we can.

INTENTIONAL STEPS
TOWARD STRENGTHENING YOURSELF

As we know, you first must love yourself to love others with a generous, strong spirit. Following the steps and exercises below provides "checks and balances" to ensure that you are nourishing and supporting yourself in all possible ways.

Step One: Let Go of Guilt

Guilt, the superpower of motherly emotions, is a force to be reckoned with. Knowingly or unknowingly, we allow guilt to shape our lives. We are making decisions about everything under the sun using our guilt as the compass by which we chart our family's path. Time and time again, women I spoke with mentioned guilt. And they did so casually, as if their guilt was as innate a part of motherhood as their love for their children. It is this guilt-induced fog that keeps us from our true selves and desires and from making healthy, sound decisions. Psychologist Harriet Lerner, author of *The Mother Dance*, describes the mother-guilt phenomenon: "Try to remember that our society encourages mothers to cultivate guilt like a little flower garden, because nothing blocks the awareness and expression of legitimate anger as effectively as this all-consuming emotion. . . . Guilt keeps mothers narrowly focused on the question 'What's wrong with me?' and prevents us from becoming effective agents of personal and social change."

Guilt comes in all shapes and sizes: The mother who doesn't allow herself time to exercise, because she'd leave her child for 45 minutes. The part-time transcriber who works from 10:00 P.M. to 2:00 A.M. so she doesn't take time away from her children, just her much-needed sleep. The working mother who doesn't ask her husband for help with the nighttime ritual, because she's feeling guilty being away from her children most of the day. Or the physical therapist, administrative assistant, lawyer, jewelry maker, or accounting manager who has put her career on hold to "do the right thing," according to cultural definitions of what motherhood means.

In addition to the guilt mothers feel over "doing too much," outside of the home, there is corresponding guilt over sidelining personal goals and financial independence. In a poignant article on Salon.com, Cecelie S. Berry writes about her women's book club: "Once determined careerists, we are now at-home mothers, each of us with at least two children. We feel splintered and disenfranchised from a culture of paid, working parents, who, whatever they say, think we have it easy. . . . Fueling our discomfort is the perception that staying at home with our children is a betrayal of our professional training. After all, you don't need a degree to be an at-home mother. . . . I'll never forget the parting comment of one of my Harvard Law School class-

The Guilt Barometer

How much time do you spend feeling guilty? Is your guilt about work, relationships with others, tasks, money, loss of self, time constraints, and so forth? List all of the items about which you feel guilty, and rate the guilt from 1 to 10, 10 being the highest level of guilt, based on intensity of feeling. Is this guilt appropriate, healthy guilt, or the inappropriate and aptly named toxic guilt?

- Healthy guilt is the normal guilt we feel when we've messed up. Healthy guilt comes up when you snap at your children when you're really mad at yourself, or when you're late picking them up from school. It comes from a real slipup for which you are accountable.
- Toxic guilt is when we take inappropriate emotional responsibility for another person's happiness. It is toxic guilt if you feel guilty that your child is whining about not having ice cream for breakfast. When you're leaving the kids with a babysitter to go out with your husband for the first time in a month—and the kids are complaining, and you feel like a bad parent. This is toxic guilt.

mates: 'Don't worry about which area to practice,' he said. 'Soon you'll be home changing diapers.'" Berry explains, "My life is a revolution, interrupted."

Step Two: Get Rid of Your Mother Martyr

Guilt has birthed one of the most enduring and tenacious female legacies around—the Mother Martyr, an archetypal example of the ideally devoted mother. Trying to plan for the birth of our second child, I had the brilliant idea of providing room and board for a college student in the spare room in our basement—not a glamorous setting, but sunny and private—in exchange for about 12 hours a week as a mother's helper. I imagined being able to care for my newborn and 3-year-old, while feeling rested, having an organized house, exercising, and working a couple of hours a day. With a bit of help cleaning, cooking, and caretaking both children, this would all be possible.

Because I knew how difficult having a newborn was, I was determined to create a support system that would promote sanity. My first child had been high need, and I didn't sleep more than 3 consecutive hours (on a good night!) for the first year. I should have been arrested for driving under the influence of sleeplessness. I was a maniac, for someone who's normally pretty even-keeled, and realized that the entire concept of sitting home raising a child alone was nuts. Where was my support system, my extended family, my tribe? If I could have recreated Anita Diamant's lovely vision from her book, *The Red Tent*, of a tent full of supportive women in my backyard, I would have woven the red canvas and harvested the tent stakes myself.

For this new baby, and because Gill was working long hours away from home, I wanted to create a web of support—something I felt that I, and every new parent, deserved. It all came crashing down when in a rush of excitement I explained my plan to my mother. "Wouldn't it be wonderful," I said, "if I weren't on the verge of a physical and emotional breakdown with this new baby?" My mother's simple, dead-serious response was, "But that's motherhood. It's about suffering." Mother Martyr emboldened, she looked at me, and immediately I felt inadequate. I was a wimp. I was betraying all Mother Martyrs before me. I didn't love my children enough, because I wasn't willing to sacrifice myself on the stake of suffering. Bottom line, I was just not a good mother.

Sounds ridiculous, doesn't it? And yet, as devoted as we are to our children, many of us are just as committed to the Mother Martyr. The Mother Martyr echoes in our head, doing her best to derail us at all times, encouraging us to criticize others for their choices and perpetuating guilt, suffering, and unquestioning self-sacrifice. Christina, a stay-at-home mom, humorously relays the message her mother passed on to her about parenting: "You sacrifice yourself for the good of the children, but then you make your kids feel very guilty about it." She explains, "My mom was a single mom who worked full-time, and an extreme level of guilt always pervaded our household. If she stayed home from work to take care of me, there was guilt. If she had to go to work to support me, there was guilt."

Yet Christina admits that she herself does a poor job of taking care of her own needs as a mother. "I definitely don't take care of myself in general. I'm trying to exercise once a week now. Trying to look for other fulfillment outside of the home, continuing education, classes, time with friends." But when pressed, she admits she hasn't signed up for any classes and does something probably less than once a month on her own with friends. She also gently teases another mother at the interview group who exercises every day and does take care of her-

Oh, Mother Martyr, Wherefore Art Thou?

Images of the long-suffering one, noble and brave, are everywhere. To help you identify which Mother Martyrs have most strongly influenced you, ask yourself (possibly with a girlfriend) the following questions.

- Who are some of the most famous Mother Martyrs, in television, films, and history?
- Who are the Mother Martyrs in your life?
- What are their primary messages?
- What Mother Martyr philosophies have you adopted subconsciously or consciously?
- What Mother Martyr phrases run through your head?

When we're embodying the Mother Martyr, we're not parenting from a place of strength and love, but rather guilt and suffering. Remember why the Mother Martyr needs to be cast off.

- It's not noble to be long-suffering. This doesn't make us better parents, better spouses, or more important.
- Our decisions shouldn't be driven by toxic guilt; we are not responsible for the emotional well-being of everyone around us.
- Don't encourage Mother Martyr competition among friends. Identify it when it starts to happen, and recognize that there are ways to diffuse it. Support each other in developing your interior and exterior lives as women through exercise, personal growth, and career development.

self. Unwittingly, Christina's mother's legacy has been passed along to her, and despite her protests, she has also taken on the burden of the Mother Martyr, queen of suffering and sacrifice.

Sometimes, it's necessary to perform Mother Martyr interventions. One of my close friends, a stay-at-home mom, has kids the same age as mine. She was so sleep deprived that she had lost rational thought and couldn't see what a rut she was in. I announced that it was time for a Mother Martyr Intervention and that she needed to take care of herself. She agreed she needed help, and exactly 2 days later, we were on our way to buy beauty products at a department store and spend a day at our local pool just reading, talking, and relaxing.

Be careful not to confuse the Mother Martyr with the normal compromises and sacrifices of parenting. As a friend, Ellen, says, "If I chose to do more things for myself, it would cut down on my productivity and I'd make less money, and I couldn't afford Jake's special school." Her son is autistic, and it's important to her that Jake attends a school that specializes in working with autistic kids. "There are consequences to my choices," she points out. "I'm very willing to work hard and carpool my kids halfway around the country, but I still maintain a few things for myself: work that I love; an amazing group of women friends; and twice a year, a vacation with my husband— alone!" Even though Ellen has made compromises and continues to sacrifice gladly for her children, she holds onto what's most important to maintaining her sense of self.

Step Three: Let Go of Control; Let Go of Worry

Kimberly, a high-energy mother of two, called me on the telephone with a classic complaint: Why am *I* always the one who takes off from work to take my kids to the doctor? She was fuming mad, not because she had to take her kindergarten son to the doctor for an ear infection, pick up a prescription, and stay home with him for the day. She knew that caring for her son was more important than her work at that moment. Kimberly just didn't understand why her husband didn't feel that tending to their son's health was more important than his job. "With two kids, I've probably been to the doctor 30 to 40 times in the last 5 years—for regular checkups, sick visits, immunizations—and in that time Gary has been once. And that's only because I made him do it!" During most of the 5 years since having children, they both had comparable jobs earning high salaries. But now Kimberly worked at home doing high-level marketing consulting with demanding clients. Whether or not she worked in an office or at home, though, she had automatically become the sick-child caretaker.

When I asked Kimberly if she and her husband had ever prenegotiated arrangements for handling work-interrupting events such as sick children and doctor's appointments, she admitted that they hadn't. "And usually it just becomes this major argument in the heat of the moment. I'm driving a sick child, having to reschedule a client meeting on my cell phone, getting more and more pissed off at my husband, who has no sympathy for the situation." It's difficult for us to be sympathetic to others when their realities bear no relation to our own. In Kimberly's case, it was hard for her husband to have sympathy while bearing the brunt of Kimberly's frustration and anger, when he, in fact, had never had to juggle work and sick children as she had. Revealingly, she ended the conversation with a personal insight. "Even if my husband took the kids to the doctor, I would probably still want to go, because I know I should. I just don't know that I could trust him to ask the right questions, describe the symptoms, or listen well enough. I mean, I would *have* to know that stuff—and would Gary really pay attention?"

Like Kimberly, many women I spoke with confessed to being control freaks when it comes to their house and children. Susan Braun-Levine calls it gatekeeping in her book *Father Courage*. Peggy Orenstein calls it mother management in her book *Flux*. Whatever you name it, our inability to let go of control while simultaneously resenting our partner's lack of contribution can be toxic to our relationships. It doesn't exactly nurture trust, either.

Just as we cannot cede control, there seems to be a tape recorder implanted in our subconscious repeating messages about what we "should do, because I'm the mother." We believe that we are *supposed* to be in charge, we are *supposed* to have the most important, if not only, major bond with the child, and if the child is bonding with someone else—even if it's the father, even if it's temporary—we question our legitimacy as mothers. It's hard to let go of control, as the gatekeepers and mother managers can attest. It's hard to open ourselves up to rejection from our children, criticism from family and friends, and the nasty judge in our minds.

Many of us believe that we are truly better parents than our mates and only reluctantly allow them to solo parent. A nervous stay-at-home mom describes, "I fear for my child's safety, because I know that when I leave my husband and son together alone, my son may have more bumps and bruises when I return. He doesn't anticipate the fall, the sharp corner, the door jam finger crush, like I do." A pension consultant and mother of school-age children in their early teens remarked, "My husband can be preoccupied and not in tune with the emotional needs of our children. I notice if they withdraw to their rooms and into their own heads and see that they may have had a rough time at school. I would know how to approach them, but my husband often has the attitude that they can deal with it themselves. I don't think he understands that he can emotionally hurt and alienate them by not being inquisitive or sensitive."

Assuming that we're better parents than our mates just because we're women, and that men are somehow inadequate in the parenting department, flies in the face of equal parenting and sabotages men's parenting ability.

So why do we assume that fathers are lacking the emotional and empathetic skills to parent as sensitively as women? There is certainly an anthropological bias. As Pepper Schwartz describes in her book, *Peer Marriage*, "It is easy to see why tender feelings might have traditionally been discouraged in men. Men have always been asked to do the hard thing: go to battle, fight for economic survival, protect the family from enemies and natural disaster. Too soft a nature might get in the way of these hard decisions and acts." Yet many women describe partners who are more nurturing and tender than themselves. A graphic artist explains, "After my son was born, I was totally awkward with the baby. It was like, 'What do I do with this scrawny, fragile little thing?' But my husband was so comfortable and sweet. I was shocked at how natural he was with the baby—and how unnatural it was for me. Still, now that my son is four, my husband is closer to him than I am. It's both physical and emotional. He's just a better parent than I am, I think."

Buying into the myth of mother as sole nurturer keeps us in emotional paralysis. It can foster a lack of trust in our own partners, most of who deserve our trust, and result in low expectations—for our own lives, for our marriages, and of our husbands. And here is the simple truth: More fathering does not mean less mothering. In fact, encouraging closeness and bonding between children and fathers is the ultimate in confident, loving mothering. Consciously letting go of

Give Up Control

If children teach us one thing it is this: Life is out of our control. We cannot predict the sudden fever that requires us to cancel a weekend camping trip. We cannot anticipate the hurt feelings that needed tending to while dinner burned. We cannot know that our teenage daughter will experiment with drugs. And we cannot keep a family vacation free of bad weather and stomach flu. Sometimes lack of predictability leads us to control all the little things, such as how the table is set, the laundry folded, and the bed made.

There are things that are worth controlling, such as what food is in the refrigerator, how much television the children watch, and that they get to school on time. And it's nice to have some level of control around the home, such as having a sanitary bathroom and clean clothes to wear. But if we endeavor to overmanage every aspect of our lives, we will be sorely disappointed—and stressed out! Let go. . . .

control and worry in the different areas of your life, including housework and child care, is one of the most important aspects to equal parenting. If control is do-or-die for you, this will be one of your biggest challenges. If you are like me, letting go of control will be a relief as sweet as the sound of your 2-year-old calling for Daddy in the night instead of Mommy.

Step Four: Value Your Dreams and Goals

Mothering may be the most important and meaningful work we do, but it doesn't solely define us, nor should it be our only calling. We get so caught up in making everyone else's dreams come true, we can forget our own. It's our responsibility as mothers to continue on—or begin—the path of our mission in life, modeling for our children how to be happy adults. Yes, many times parenting demands sacrifice and compromise. Perhaps it makes sense for you to stop working or pare down to part-time while your children are small; but doesn't it also make sense for your husband to share this responsibility? Putting off more schooling or career development may be the right choice for you now, but it's important that it's only on hold, not forgotten.

Angela, a passionate, curious, and creative mother of one, felt enervated after almost 20 years as a dance instructor. "I love dance, but it's hard on my body to teach full-time, and I'm burned out. I need to focus on what I love, which is teaching children, and get a teaching credential, but it's scary. For a long time, I used my child as an excuse not to take this next step, but now that she's in school, I need to face this." When we become mired in the routine of child care—bedtime rituals, meals, and school schedules—sometimes change seems as likely an option as climbing Mt. Everest. We forget the exhilaration that change can bring and the sense of pride we feel when mastering new skills. Angela, now in a 12-month program to get her teaching credential, says she feels alive again. She's reconnected with her passion for teaching and feels powerful accomplishing her goals.

Our dreams and goals should not be taken lightly. They are different than the dreams we have for our children; they're the dreams we hold onto for ourselves. They fill us up and make us complete people—whether we dream of running a half-marathon, getting a real estate license, or being promoted at work. My sister-in-law, Robin, directs the musicals at her children's elementary school with the organization and verve of a Broadway producer: Her three kids love her involvement, participate in the musicals, and see their mother in a new

The Goals and Dreams Interview

Ask the questions now, so you can live the answers later. Perhaps your goal is to interact with people, manage an office, work on a computer, read, write, or study. Maybe your goal is to participate in a personal growth seminar, volunteer at a women's shelter, or learn a new exercise or sport. If you are clear about your dreams, you're one step ahead. Many of us don't have a clue. So ask yourself, what are you missing? In what environment do you thrive? What time in your life or place has felt personally fulfilling? What are your secret—or not so secret—dreams and goals? Place no limitations on your abilities. Imagine this next exercise, with all the bells and whistles.

Barbara Walters is conducting an exclusive interview with you—but 10 years from now. In her personal, engaging style, she asks you these very important questions. What will your answers be? What would you like your future to look like?

- You're radiant; you're glowing. What have you been doing physically to take such good care of yourself?
- Let's talk about your accomplishments. Besides motherhood—which all moms know is their crowning achievement—what are you most proud of?
- Motherhood is filled with joyful moments but also challenges. Explain what it feels like to have overcome some of the obstacles in your way.
- How are you different than you were a decade ago? Are you more confident? More world-weary? Have your priorities shifted?
- What are the highlights you've experienced since becoming a mother? What goals have been met, and what are your new dreams?

light in which she shines. Linda, a 46-year-old mother and jewelry maker, competes in triathlons: Her two teenage daughters couldn't be more proud when their mother crosses the finish line. Wenda, mother of one daughter, holds an accounting position at a major firm, which has been her lifelong goal. As an immigrant to the United States in her early twenties, who spoke little English, she is filled with pride at her achievements—and vigilant about showing her daughter that hard work and positive attitudes make dreams come true.

When you are on the path to achieving your goals—when you're passionate, engaged, and proud—your children will feel the same way. The great byproduct of honoring our dreams and goals is that it teaches our children how to achieve their goals.

Step Five: Take Care of Your Physical and Emotional Needs

The other day at the gym, my friend Eve relayed a story from her neighbor who has a 5-year-old, gregarious daughter, "I was making dinner, and I overheard my little girl and her two friends talking about their mothers. It was all I could do to keep quiet when my daughter announced, 'My mom has a monkey between her legs.' If that's not great imagery for what happens to your body after giving birth to three children, I don't know what is!" The monkey line literally brought me to my knees, and I was on the floor in stitches, in the middle of the weight room.

Mothering changes not only the structure of our daily lives, but our bodies and our interior lives as well. Some of us spring back into our old jeans in a matter of months, but most of us do not. It's not just childbirth and the beginning of motherhood that takes its toll, it's years of putting others' physical and emotional needs first. Women are excellent at finding excuses for why they cannot take care of themselves. As Becky says, "I work so much, how can I, in good conscience, exercise or do anything besides be with my kids?" It is not simply about looking good in jeans, though. Inertia doesn't help anyone. In a *Ms. Magazine* article, Mariah Burton Nelson says, "The more women play sports, the more they respect themselves, stand up for themselves, team up with other women, and perhaps also refuse to tolerate abuse. . . . The more women gain physical and emotional strength, the less feasible it is for men to treat women as inferior."

We also neglect our emotional health. Depression and feelings of self-doubt hit some mothers hard. Lilia, mother of a 10-year-old and a 6-month-old new baby, found herself unable to return to work running her own small business, because her depression was so severe. "I have three sisters, all with children, and none of them had postpartum or any kind of depression that I knew of. I thought something was wrong with me, so I checked myself into the hospital and had tests run. The doctor told me that physically I was fine, but that mentally, I needed to get support from a professional. I couldn't believe it. I told my sisters, and they all came to help me—and I realized that I was overwhelmed with my life and my business, and the tears started and didn't stop for about 2 weeks. It was a great relief." Once Lilia got help from her family and some time for herself, she began to come out of her depression (her hormones leveled out as well). But it's not easy. Some women spend years at home or doing double duty as working moms, only to find themselves on the floor, a heap of extreme exhaustion with little self-esteem. Don't wait until you're flat out to do something.

When you take your own needs seriously, you stand on an emotional platform of strength, love, and purpose rather than resentment, anger, or confusion. It's not okay to sacrifice everything—including your sanity—for your family. Taking care of yourself must become a matter of priority. After lots of harassment from my husband, I am learning to choose exercise over other things, because it makes such an immediate and profound difference in how I feel. It makes me feel stronger in all ways. I can do anything after exercise. So, if I've sacrificed a trip to the grocery store or a playdate for my child, or walked during my lunch hour instead of eating at my desk while working, too bad. My children and husband will reap the rewards of a strong, happy mom. From this place of physical and

Ask Yourself: Body Questions

Janice, the mother of three teenagers, hadn't been physically active since her second child was born 15 years earlier. Formerly a college athlete, sports were very important in her family's life, as she shuttled everyone from one practice to another, one game to another. "I feel so out of touch with myself as a former athlete that it seems like another time. It *was* another time! But I vividly remember what it feels like to run down the soccer field, strong and capable. It helps you feel stronger in your life, sexier, better about everything. It's hard for me to believe that I haven't even gone to the gym in 15 years. Wow."

The more out of touch we are with our bodies, the more our confidence and sexuality are affected. Ask yourself the following questions and journal the answers if you have time.

- How has your relationship with your body changed since having children?
- Did childbirth help you come to a new level of appreciation for your body?
- What can you do to get back in touch with your sexuality?

mental strength, the best parenting, the best marriage, the strongest family can flower.

Final Step: Create Goals for a Stronger Self

Many of us get caught up in the practicalities of motherhood, focusing on the details: Do my children have proper clothing, are they well-fed, read to, socializing with other children? In other words, have I, the mother, provided a healthy, stimulating environment for my child? But this constant outward focus doesn't encourage us to judge whether we provide such an exemplary environment for ourselves. Giving our children the gift of a resourceful, independent, engaged, passionate woman who is also a happy mother is just as important to their sense of well-being as a warm jacket on a chilly day. Of course, the details of parenting are important. But just as powerful are the moments, few and far between, that I can remember when my mother did things for herself. The times she bought a new outfit and dressed up for a party, spent time with a friend, or had a part-time job that gave her purpose. In these moments I saw another face of my mother, someone that I wanted to know more of. Someone who was strong, capable, and joyful. I admired my mom, I thought she was beautiful, and I was happy knowing that she was fulfilled. Children don't want their mothers to sacrifice themselves, their identities, their bodies, and their interests. Like the child who complained, "I wish that my mom's career wasn't me!" they want whole people as mothers.

How can you be a strong, fulfilled woman? Look at all the areas in your life, and set goals to ensure that you nurture yourself and your own interests. Don't overcommit. Don't set yourself up to be superhuman. Don't define your priorities as what you think they should be; define them as what you need. Here are some areas to consider.

Overall Goals

Physical Health: What kind of physical activity and health maintenance do you need in order to feel good? Remember to consider exercise needs and physical health.

 ❋ Join a gym, take a class, or walk 30 minutes a day.

 ❋ Learn a new sport or activity.

 ❋ Set goals for physical health and maintenance.

Emotional Health: Mothering guarantees that your heart is ripped wide open. Be vigilant about nurturing tenderness, explore confusion, and don't ignore the dark side.

 ❋ Join or start a mother's group or visit mothering Web sites and chat boards for support.

 ❋ Keep a journal and write 10 minutes every day.

 ❋ Continue or explore a spiritual or meditation practice.

Grooming and Pampering: As Billy Crystal said on *Saturday Night Live*, "It's not how you *feel*, it's how you *look!*" It may seem trivial, but don't underestimate the importance of TLC.

 ❋ Get a manicure, facial, or special treatment.

 ❋ Maintain your hairstyle and color.

 ❋ Enjoy a massage.

Career Development: Dedicate yourself to short- and long-term plans. Jumpstart your brain, creative energy, and drive.

 ❋ Explore a college continuing education course locally or via the Internet.

❋ Join a writer's group, investment club, or book discussion group to keep up-to-date with your skills and cultural awareness.

Friendships: Friends keep us laughing and sane. (It's particularly important to choose some friends with great wit.) How can you choose to be around positive, supportive people?
  ❋ Connect with old friends via e-mail or letters.
  ❋ Plan girls' night out with other friends once a month.
  ❋ Deepen friendships and consider who to call on for support with parenting and other advice.

Community Service: Most of us have very little time, but it may be important to you to be on the PTA board or run for local (state or federal!) government. You can enact change.
  ❋ Get involved with your local school, church, or other volunteer organization.
  ❋ Choose one or two issues that are meaningful to you—such as breast cancer research or the environment—and consider how to contribute.

NEGOTIATION POINTS

The negotiation points in this chapter are unique, because they are exclusively for the mother. They should be called "nonnegotiable" items instead, for these are the first things that most women discard after having children—to the detriment of themselves and their families. Remember, we owe it to ourselves and our families to take care of our emotional, physical, and intellectual needs. There will be times when it's impossible—sick children, work commitments, or an over-committed life—but if you make your well-being a priority by discarding the baggage of guilt and the Mother Martyr, you can use the negotiation points as a checklist and action plan to make time and care for yourself.

Need: What and How	Timeframe
Physical Health	
Physical activity plan	
Exercising	
Time in nature	
Stretching	
Doctors appointments	
Regular checkups	
Chronic or acute issues	
Alternative medicine	
Body work	
Ongoing maintenance	
Emotional Health	
Support groups for mothers	
Therapy	
Church groups	
Meditations	
Career Development (see also chapter 4)	
Take classes	
Informational interviews	
Talk with your manager about opportunities	

Need: What and How	Timeframe
Create career time line for change or advancement	
Network in your industry	
Friendships	
Activities with women friends	
Dinner out	
Weekend away	
Concert, book signing, exercise class	
Write e-mails to keep in touch	
Combine playdates with moms	
Grooming and Pampering	
Haircuts, hair color, hairdos	
Body treatments	
Massage	
Spa time	
Waxing, plucking, shaping	
Shopping for clothes	
Shopping for beauty products	
Community Service	
Volunteering	
School	
Local or national politics	
Parent organizations	
Hobbies:	
Sports	
Reading	
Writing	
Arts	
Classes	

INTENTION: COMMIT TO SELF-LOVE AND TAKING CARE OF YOURSELF

Many times I have wanted to throw my hands up and scream, "Forget it!" I have felt like resigning myself to what amounts to loss: the loss of my partner being more formally involved in raising our children; the loss to our children of being with their father more; the loss to society of men sensitive to family and child-related issues. It's the depth of these losses that kicks me in the pants and reminds me why it's so important to be in a parenting partnership and not settle for inequality. When you commit to choosing what works best for your family and to honoring yourself, there are no losers, only stronger families, better marriages, and happier mothers.

As you embark on this new path, it's important to stay grounded in reality and in your own truth and to develop techniques to find your way back—whether through music, affirmations, time with friends, books, or walks in nature. I have my own ritual: Often at the end of a long day of work and parenting that started at 5:30 A.M., I put on music, play it loud, and do a little dancing to one of my "power songs." Sometimes it's Tori Amos or Tracy Chapman, and other times it's 4 Non Blondes or Bonnie Raitt. Just hearing the strength of these voices and moving my body to the music reinvigorates my own voice and determination. Almost always, my daughter is dancing by my side, in a flouncy princess outfit or ballet leotard, pumping her little fists. After the songs end, she yells out, "Mom, I want another power song!" I see my husband and son in the living room wings, grinning and watching the females of the house dance; Gill knows that a new era has been ushered in—and it makes me sing even louder.

Finding Your Power Place

We all have methods we use, consciously or not, to reconnect with our inner strength. For some it's taking a walk, knitting, or talking with your best friend. Develop a practice to find your way back to your center when you lose faith and direction. Give yourself permission to use this tool often. Here are some suggestions.

- Music can speak to your soul and likewise help your soul find its voice again. Sing out loud.
- Journaling about your emotions and experiences can release, illuminate, and fortify. Write what you feel.
- Moving our bodies can move our minds. Walk, dance, swim, or whack a tennis ball.
- Creative expression frees our unique talents and our unspoken emotions. Spend time with a camera or a paintbrush, and let your artistic self out.
- Silence and loneliness is underrated (as mothers know). Spend time alone breathing stillness.

Strengthening Yourself Intention Statement:

I commit to strengthening myself by loving and taking care of myself.

I value myself and realize that my dreams, goals, and identity are not worth sacrificing.

_____
Signed

63

Loving Each Other

"The heart is a living museum. In each of its galleries,
no matter how narrow or dimly lit,
preserved forever like wondrous diatoms,
are moments of loving and being loved."

–Diane Ackerman, *A Natural History of Love*

Sometimes a romantic partnership works so well it's like an Olympic gymnast's perfect vault. It's beautiful. A flawless 10. Our personalities and quirks have contorted to fit together seamlessly, and our relationship, through woes and rough spots, succeeds with strength, grace, and dexterity. And then we flub. In an instant, our love turns clumsy. We trip on the takeoff, the mat comes up and grabs us, and the chalk for our hands turns into war paint. We skulk. We seethe. Suddenly, we're strangers, competitors, and the loving partnership that felt so right feels impossibly far away.

You have, I hope, experienced those perfect moments with your partner, moments when the two of you are perfectly in sync, chemistry on a rolling boil, love prevailing. Most of the time, though, our relationships don't rate a perfect 10, because one or both partners is suffering—emotionally or physically. The true test of any relationship

Loving Each Other Quiz

I often look at young married couples longingly. "Remember when that was us, Honey?" I ask nostalgically. But what these young couples really represent is an idyllic romantic time, a time when we explored the possibilities of our relationship, our life together, and our future. We had the luxury of time and freedom to be obsessive about "us." Now that dreamy, self-involved time is filled by the practical concerns of loving and caring for our children and family environment. Now, instead of drifting into a night of intimacy or long, meandering conversations about our relationship, we must be intentional and specific about connecting. Easier said than done, I know. The questions below will help you evaluate the current status of your connection with your partner.

1. Do you feel that you and your partner are in harmony with family priorities? Couple priorities? Personal priorities? Financial priorities?
2. What ways do you communicate unhappiness or anger to each other?

occurs when we are not our best selves. Enter parenting. "Research has shown that on the average, the greatest challenge to a couple is becoming parents. Many marriages hold together for a few years when the child is young, but they've been strained beyond repair by everything that comes from having kids, and the couple divorces, maybe by the time the kid reaches first grade," says psychologist Rick Hanson, author of *Mother Nurture*. Given the strain parenting places on our relationships, how can we still treat each other well when we're exhausted? When work stress is high? When parenting is hardest? When we cannot rise to these everyday challenges, we can find ourselves coexisting in an altered relationship state that can be permanently fixed on dull, contentious, or downright horrible.

3. Do you feel that your needs and emotions are taken seriously? Are you able to laugh with each other?

4. Do you talk about sex?

5. Describe your sex life. Is it thriving, varied, full of love or gentleness? Is it a distant memory, exhausting, or comfortably predictable?

6. What are your biggest recurring arguments about? Have you actively tried to overcome these issues?

7. Is there something for which you haven't been able to forgive your spouse? Some way in which you find your spouse inconsolable?

8. When was the last time you discussed politics? A book? An event?

9. When was the last time you felt happy to be together at a cultural event, dancing, playing a sport? Just being together?

10. What do you like most about each other's interests and passions?

11. Have you discussed ways to support each other's physical health, sleep, nutrition, or emotional well-being?

One of the best gifts we can give our children is to love our partners—deeply, truly, and passionately. A strong, loving alliance tells children that we will be there for them, that they can count on our love and support, because our marriage is stable and not going away. In our idyllic moments, we can model how to love, how to value differences, and how to respect others. Our actions can demonstrate generosity, loving-kindness, and reciprocity. In our imperfect moments, we can teach them how to disagree, argue, and work though it. It's these examples of discussion and compromise that may, in fact, give our children the most enduring skills needed in life: how to peacefully work through both internal and external conflict.

Quick Tips

If you feel disconnected and in need of urgent care, here are four things in this chapter that might have the most immediate impact.

1. Take the "Loving Each Other Quiz" at the beginning of the chapter (page 66) to identify key problem areas.
2. Go to the "Expressing Your Love" exercise on page 75 to understand where you have come from and where you want to go.
3. Go to "Defusing Anger" on page 80, and have a heart-to-heart talk about how you express anger in your relationship.
4. Make your relationship a priority by taking an active step: Plan a getaway from your children to spend time focusing solely on each other.

YOUR CHANGING RELATIONSHIP

As Germaine Greer says, "A successful marriage requires falling in love many times, always with the same person." And when we become parents, our changing relationship offers newer, deeper ways to love our partners. Children expand our relationships, as we discover new qualities in each other. "My husband's love for our children makes me melt sometimes," a 41-year-old sales manager and mother of three says. "His commitment to the family, and the joy he gets from loving our children, is extraordinary. He's nurturing, emotionally present, playful, and protective. I adore him all over again!"

Couples rise to the occasion of parenthood, strengthening their relationship to meet the structural demands of family life, as a 24-year-old stay-at-home mother explains: "I think we are even more in love since our daughter was born, because we have had to let go of some of our barriers and issues in order to make our family work. Our issues—such as sharing housework—pale in comparison with the love for our child. Now we're even better at not blaming each other for things, and our commitment to being calm and willing to go with the flow is even stronger."

Our hearts are made vulnerable when children arrive. Sarah, mother of grown children, explains, "Emotionally, the miracle of parenthood is overwhelming. You cannot prepare for something as amazing as a child. I didn't know that I would be so in love with someone, other than my spouse, ever. It was truly beautiful. I do think because of the daily needs of the child, your spouse unfortunately can end up taking a back seat. I don't want that to happen all of the time, and we do try to make time for ourselves. It's much easier now that our

How We Feel about Our Relationships

The carefree days of courtship and romance may seem like ancient history. But you are still the person your partner fell in love with, and vice versa. Revisit, through conversation, your relationship before kids.

- What did you love about your relationship in the beginning?
- What was your favorite weekend activity? Your regular restaurant or coffee shop?
- Remember a favorite vacation or weekend away.
- What qualities and activities do you miss most in your relationship?
- What do you wish you could get back?

kids are older. We've even gotten away for weekends, and a special 20th anniversary trip to Maui—all without the kids." Explaining that their love isn't as passionate but is strong and steady, she elaborates, "I am not sad with the changes; I see it as a natural evolution of our relationship. His love and devotion to the kids and myself hasn't wavered, but sometimes the little things slip—like thoughts of appreciation, and so on. And there are moments that one of us is doing more than the other, and I know I want to be recognized for that sacrifice. But in the long run, for us at least, it all comes together in the love we share within our family."

HOW ARE WE STRUGGLING?

Twice last week, women called me asking for the name of a great couples therapist I know. At the park, I struck up a conversation with a woman watching over her toddler, and she confessed she hadn't had sex with her husband for almost a year; when I told a friend about this story, she grudgingly admitted that she and her husband hadn't been intimate for several months. Over and over again, I have heard people admit that they are settling for a relationship that is less than adequate, where passion has fizzled out. Often they rationalize that this is a change couples must accept as the price they pay for being parents. Certainly, our love for our partners hasn't vanished into thin air. But parents, formerly known as couples, seem to be struggling everywhere I turn. While we are showering our children with love and attention, we, as couples, suffer a severe drought of affection for each other and ourselves. Many of us are stuck in a pattern of roughshod communication, little intimacy, and zero couple time. One or both partners may be tapped out—emotionally, physically, or psychologically.

Jenna was a manager at a software company and had two children, ages six and eight. With flex time and working at home 1 day a week, she felt like she was able to be there for her kids when they needed her—but her husband, an accountant, worked long hours and had a 2-hour-a-day commute. I was hoping to finally interview Jenna by telephone, since she had scheduled and cancelled two previous interviews. But when she answered her phone, I could immediately tell that she didn't have the time to talk. "Do you want to reschedule? Are you sure you even want to talk?" I asked. She was adamant. "The reason I don't have time to talk to you is precisely why it's important that I do talk to you," she said.

It was only noon, but she explained her day to me: "Today is one of those days when motherhood feels hopeless: This morning, I got my kids ready for school by myself as usual, since my husband leaves at 6:30. I see my first-grader has a clear, runny nose—and he complains that his throat is scratchy. They were just sick! I feel major pressure to go to work, and I know that if he stays home, so do I. So I'm weighing my need to work versus my guilt sending a sick kid to school. And while I'm going through this emotional arm wrestling— ALL on a Monday morning before I've even started my official workday—my husband has no idea what's going on. He is never forced to make these decisions or sacrifices, nor does he feel an ounce of guilt. I don't get how he can check out this way; it puts tremendous pressure on me, and then I turn around and put my anger on him. And of course I stayed home." I sympathized with Jenna and asked her how this affected her marriage.

"Very timely, this question. We had a huge fight last night with Greg summarizing, 'Our life is just not any fun.' Fun?! I wanted to lay into him for being so selfish. I'd settle for boring and predictable. Who could hope for fun? I'm despairing because here I am a feminist married to a decent guy who loves his family but is clueless about what it really takes to run the family and household, and I do everything. Plus we do have fun—on vacations, on the weekends—but it's the day to day that's so hard." I pressed her to tell me about the emotional temperature of her relationship. "I'm so irritable and angry, and that comes between us. Other times I feel guilty for being difficult. I also realize that there is no easy fix and that my husband is trying to do the best he can. It's impossibly hard to figure this stuff out, and because we're in such a tug-of-war over it, our marriage is a real downer sometimes. I know that I don't just want to accept it and resign myself. That feels like quitting and giving up."

Later that evening, Jenna leaves a message on my answering machine to apologize for her complaints (a perfect example of women always feeling as if they have to apologize for being frustrated with their domestic situation.) "I had a horrible start to the day, but it got much better. I spent the day with my son reading and baking and watching a video—and my husband called to say how much he appreciates what I do for our kids and that our life is wonderful together. I appreciate his words—and I know it's not easy for him either." She did mention that her boss was frustrated with her and she was feeling pressure about work, but for the time being she was feeling at peace with the choices she was making for her family.

Resentment, anger, confusion, guilt—all of the feelings that Jenna expresses are common to most parents and can create walls; some we can scale and others keep us apart. Resentment takes many forms: seething anger, annoyance, irritability, passive-aggressive behavior, superficial niceties. And it wells up for different reasons: overworking all the time or not working enough; over the division of household chores and lack of parenting involvement; over career choices and financial decisions; over lack of intimacy and becoming second fiddle to children.

For some women, such as Susan, the resentment is minor, "My only complaint is that I don't get enough—or sometimes any—free time on the weekends. I feel like my partner should do more alone with our daughter on the weekends. I think he would if I asked him to, but it just usually works out that he has more things he wants to go do by himself than I do." Men are often better at taking care of themselves and less likely to fall into the Mother Martyr trap—sometimes to the detriment of their relationships. (See "Get Rid of Your Mother Martyr" on page 44 for how to avoid this trap.)

Other women, for whom motherhood has resulted in new, non-negotiated roles, feel even more resentment. Katherine, an art teacher, describes the situation with her husband, a musician: "We never discussed who would work more or less when we had our son. I just assumed the role of primary caretaker, with my husband showing up when he wanted, even though he didn't have a full work schedule and was very capable of sharing the parenting responsibility with me. I never insisted that he do it and felt that I was required to do it because I was the mom—yet now I have terrible anger that he doesn't help with much of anything. I can barely even express it, because I feel so upset and wonder how he can choose not to be with his son more. Doesn't he want a relationship with his child?"

The traditional role that Katherine has unintentionally adopted no longer works for most modern families, including hers. But pressures from family, friends, and community and our own internal pressures all influence our actions and feelings about parenting. Just as women feel pressure to tie their identity with motherhood and less so to a career, men feel the converse pressure to tie their identity to work, achievement, and a paycheck to support their family and less so to parenting.

It's not just emotional pressures that come to the fore when a couple becomes parents. Newer parents, especially, may neglect basic physical needs. Sleep deprivation is the pox on the relationship of new parents, one that kindles arguing, bad decision-making, and physical hardship. In search of those elusive extra hours in the day, many couples give up their exercise routines, sometimes permanently. They don't take time to stay physically active and connected to their bodies, and this often results in the loss of intimacy and sexual connectedness.

Finally, as parenting causes us to examine our perception of what raising children involves, we are presented with an entirely new set of challenges to our definitions of self. Often we find ourselves reliving the gender-determined parenting roles we thought we—both men and women—had been emancipated from. Parenting also makes us examine our role as a couple, magnifying the trouble spots already present in a marriage. Dormant issues that had been temporarily Band-Aided may emerge with a vengeance. We may begin to face and understand our own parents' failings. But because we exist in a perpetually time-challenged state, rarely spending time with each other, we simply resign ourselves to being unable to see many of these trouble spots through to clear skies. Yet with half of marriages ending in divorce, it doesn't pay to neglect our relationships. As a divorced mother of four children pointed out, "Divorce takes so much time

Expressing Your Love

So much of what we expect in relationships comes from our experiences as children watching the adults in our lives. We learned from our parents what qualities we do and don't want in our partners, and it's stored in our conscious and unconscious despite our best efforts to forge our own way. We may have had parents who were affectionate and jovial or who were dismissive and judgmental. Our parents may have had intellectual rapport yet little love. Divorce may have split parents apart, providing them a second chance to find the right match. Or they may have stayed in marriages that were toxic and unhealthy.

All of these models from your childhood—strong marriages, divorce, remarriage, parents in painful marriages—are shaping your expectations of love. To help you and your husband understand the nature of your love for each other:

- Take turns discussing the impressions of each of your parent's relationships and love for each other. Were there times that you saw your parents loving and respecting each other? What expressions of love did they use? How did it make you, the child, feel at the time? If your parents remarried, examine those relationships as well. Listen closely to the similarities and difference in how you each saw your parents' love manifest itself.
- Now discuss how you would you like your children to experience your marriage. Write down the ways that you would like your children to witness the love between you and your partner, such as greeting each other with a kiss at the end of the day, cooking and talking together while sharing a glass of wine, holding hands, and so on. Now trade notes with your partner.

and energy—working with lawyers, battling over household items, therapy, sorting out financial problems. Time that could have been better spent working on our marriage in the first place! We might have saved ourselves the trouble." She added, "We also didn't want to spend the money on therapy. Well, a divorce is far more expensive than a couple of years of marriage counseling!"

Parenting should not permanently distract us from our partners, from loving and caring for the very person with whom we wanted to become parents in the first place. Rather, parenting should inspire us to overcome our marital struggles and divine a different, stronger source for our relationship strength.

THE EQUAL PARENTING AGREEMENT TO LOVE EACH OTHER

We commit to an emotionally healthy relationship based on valuing and respecting each other.

Creating certain agreements about your relationship, especially when you and your partner feel like two half-sunk ships passing in the night, can truly help. These contracts give you a set of expectations for your relationship. Joanne, who travels for business frequently, can make it through difficult business trips, barely having a chance to speak with her husband, because she knows that every Saturday night will be date night. Their ritual, supported by their kids' favorite babysitter and the pizza delivery guy, begins with a slow walk to their favorite local Thai restaurant. They share the week's emotional highs and lows on the walk. By the time they reach the restaurant, they have cleared the relationship clutter away and are ready to spend the evening simply enjoying each other's company.

Before You Begin

Completing the steps below will help you define the tenets of your love and make specific goals to nurture marital equality and foster more marital happiness.

Define Your Couple Tradition

A friend was married in a small, charming Catholic church in a small town outside of Santa Fe, New Mexico. Although not Catholic, she agreed to wed in a Catholic ceremony, because her German fiancé was a practicing Catholic—and he had agreed to live in the United States. During the wedding ceremony, the priest digressed into a surprise monologue on the importance of wifely duties, such as the ironing, cooking, and cleaning, and the husbandly duties of provider and decision-maker for the family. My friend and I looked at each other midceremony and began stifling good-hearted laughter. Little did the priest know that her husband, who wasn't able to work in the country yet, was currently playing the wifely role—and a fine gourmet cook he was—and managing all of the household tasks, and My friend was playing husband as the sole breadwinner. They enjoyed the irony of the situation, feeling comfortable and confident in their contributions to the relationship.

Assess Your Need for Outside Approval

Shrugging off the well-intentioned pressures from our family, our churches, or our friends can be easy for some and difficult for others, depending on how much approval we need—and conversely how much we might be rebelling—from our families and peers. When I first had my daughter, my mother-in-law would make "parenting suggestions," statements about what I *should* have been doing: You should let her cry it out; you should not let her cry it out; you should not dress her so warmly; you should dress her more warmly. My head was spinning. Feeling vulnerable and insecure as a new parent, I wanted her to approve of my parenting and attempt at domesticity, so I justified my actions with weak explanations. Afterward, I would be furious with her—but really I was furious at myself. I didn't yet have confidence in my own parenting or even my marriage yet. A counselor Gill and I were seeing asked me a simple question, "Do you really need her approval for all your actions?" No, I didn't. I knew my mother-in-law loved me. I knew that even if I did things differently than her that she would continue to love me—and that first and foremost, I needed to feel confident finding my own place in parenting and my marriage, especially as we challenged the traditional roles of husband and wife, mother and father.

Our parents' good intentions and social traditions do drive us crazy. The pressure, whether subtle or overt, can feel overpowering sometimes and ridiculous at other times. Our roles as wife and husband—even marriage itself—can fall into stereotypes cast as tradition. The "shoulds" work hard to push us off course: She should cook for him, he should handle the finances, she should forego her career for a time, he should make more money even if it means seeing less of the children. It is only when we peel back and discard the layers of "shoulds"—the old wives' tales and traditions and external pressures—that we are able to clearly understand our own individual, couple, and

Our Need for Approval

Make decisions about your relationship roles using your own heart and the values of your relationship as a compass. To help you avoid the traps of tradition that don't work for you and to let social and family pressures roll off your back, ask yourself these questions:

- Do we need approval of this action?
- Why do I/we need approval?
- What can we do to feel self-love and confidence in this action so that we don't need external approval?
- How can we put up healthy boundaries to protect ourselves and avoid unwanted criticism or advice? How can we find or gather advice from those we trust?
- How can I continue to love those around me who may disagree with my choices?

When it comes to gender roles in this country, everybody has an opinion—so the sooner you discover your own true path to couple equality, the stronger your relationship and your parenting will be. Most of us want different relationships than our parents, yet with some of the best elements starring. We want depth, emotional connection, equality and honesty. We want a marriage that lasts far into the future and provides a landing pad for our children. Trust in your own instincts, intuition, and relationship needs. And when you find your relationship comfort zone, know it will certainly change, evolve, and swing like a pendulum, back and forth between the two of you.

family needs. What works for our family? What works for our relationship? What works for me?

The Ground Rules: Anger and Humor

Often anger defines the main emotional character of relationships, with humor a bit player. But anger can foster a state of paralysis without any hope of resolution.

Defusing Anger

When I was 8 months pregnant with our second child, Gill's parents offered to take our daughter for the weekend so that we could have one last hurrah. Since I was enormous, the promise of "hurrah" was amusing: Eating gave me gas, and romantic coupling would have constituted a medical miracle. So we went to a relationship workshop, knowing we were about to have our relationship's resiliency tested with two young children.

It was at this workshop that I realized how destructive some of my communication patterns were to our relationship. I routinely labeled Gill as the angry one, because his anger took a more obvious form. He raised his voice and got visibly upset. I, on the other hand, withdrew. I emotionally shut down, punishing him by not being available. We were classic examples of aggressive-aggressive behavior (Gill) and passive-aggressive behavior (me). I interrogated him with seemingly innocent questions, "So, was the train late?" when he arrived home 20 minutes late, or "How expensive are those fancy running shoes?" as I rolled my eyes and added a subtle but audible "tsk." Thankfully, we identified our most negative communication habits. The workshop leaders, Seana McGee and Maurice Taylor, also authors of the powerful relationship book *The New Couple* and cofounders of the Web site www.newcouple.com, helped us understand where we learned the anger patterns and had us share what forms of anger were most hurtful to us. It was a breakthrough for both of us.

Just recognizing the forms of anger that you are particularly adept at can be transforming. I'm a master eye-roller. Sarcasm is also a favorite technique, which can be cruel and cutting. The following list is adapted from Seana and Maurice's workshop and book. Remember, there is no hierarchy with anger. No one way of expressing it is better than the other—whether you tend toward aggressive, overt displays or are more stealthy in your attacks.

The Angry Attack is the most overt form of anger. *Name-calling* is attacking. Sometimes it's obvious, "How could you be so stupid?!" and sometimes it's subtle, like the husband who patted his wife's knee, looking into her eyes, and called her "my simple-minded sweetie." *Threatening* is also attacking, as in "You need to get over this," or "I would be happier as a single parent than staying with you," and slamming doors and banging pots and pans. *Bullying and Bossing* is the final attack method, and it can be employed with force, "Don't you dare walk out on me!" or a "Let's not get in a huff here, alright!" Expert Attackers employ all three: "Listen, Nag Queen, don't push me around, or I'm out of here!"

The Angry Sneak Attack is an aggressive form of anger slightly disguised. *Interrogating* is when you hide accusations in the form of questions: "Is that your fourth beer?" or "Isn't our marriage a priority to you?" *Cutting off* is used to shut out our partners, often when we don't want to hear what they're saying, "I'm not listening to another minute of this," or "End of discussion. That's it." *Accusing* is the fine art of the blame game—the "she did . . . no, he did" technique—that's used to deflect accountability. *Judging* is the razor-sharp method of undercutting your partner: "You're so like your mother," or "I'm just responsible and never missed a credit card payment like you."

Stealth Anger is used all the time in our society, and, as the name implies, often sneaks under the radar. *Sarcasm* and *Teasing* are employed in the name of fun, but they aren't fun at all. "You better not miss a workout, or your body fat might go up to 4 percent," or "Jeez, did you forget to take your PMS medicine today?" *Devaluing* is common in the battle of the sexes, "You're so emotional," or "You take everything personally," and "You're just not evolved enough; you don't get it." *Guilt-tripping* is a popular favorite also, as in "Sure, you can go out Friday night and abandon me and the kids," or "Other wives let their husbands have so much more fun."

Intellectualized Anger includes a couple of methods that those of us favor who are afraid to cop to our own feelings or are trying to deflect accountability. *Psychoanalyzing* is a technique that often drives people over the bend but leaves them feeling small and powerless, such as "Clearly, this is your abandonment issue; it's not really about me forgetting to show up to your parent's dinner party," or "You need to work on your boundaries with your boss." Similarly, *Lecturing* places the lecturer in a dominant position, "You're drinking too much," or "You just need to be consistent with your exercise."

Body Anger is a powerful mode of expressing anger. It can be difficult—and frustrating—to call people on it and to recognize it in yourself, as I can attest. It's walking out the door and physically (and emotionally) withdrawing. It's the silent treatment and building a steel fortress around yourself. It's rolling eyes and making facial expressions—or fixing the "stone cold" expression. It's turning your back on someone, moving to the edge of the bed to get away from your partner, and letting our body express that you're hurt, furious, devastated, or in pain.

Using Humor

Once you have identified and understand your anger patterns, you can be conscious of changing your responses. One of the best ways to diffuse anger or upset in the moment is using humor, especially with children around—when appropriate! Not humor that negates your partner's feelings. Not humor with an edge, such as sarcasm or teasing, but humor that helps you look at something in a new light and puts your conflict in perspective. It is a secret weapon that can turn ugly situations and behaviors around by turning them on their head. If we can laugh at ourselves—not at our partner—and take our life lightly when appropriate, it can make the late carpool pickup or the fact that there's no coffee when the kids wake up at 5:30 A.M. almost bearable.

It's important to use humor in the moment, not just after the fact. I have a strong childhood memory of bringing my dad a homemade milkshake. He was reading on his bed, and as I approached, I tripped over a book and the milkshake went flying across the bed, covering my dad and the bedspread in milky ice cream. Now this story is part of our family lore, and we laugh over it—but at the time, my father got angry (his work papers and bedspread *were* covered in milkshake).

If we can laugh at life's events down the road, it's an even stronger message to teach our children, and ourselves, to laugh at our missteps in the moment. Once last year, when Gill was working full-time and I was the primary caregiver at home, Gill and I were having a tense morning. He had used all the milk the evening before, even though I asked him not to, and I cannot wake up in the morning without my coffee and milk. It's hard enough getting up at 6:00 A.M. and having to be civil, parent two children, and get ready for work—but to have to do so without coffee was a cruel, cruel trick. I just couldn't get over it and kept making little comments (I was expertly employing the Stealth Anger technique!) about how he sabotaged my morning. Later that day, he called me—still grumpy—to tell me how he announced in a Monday meeting in his office: "If we don't meet our deadlines this week, I'm going to force everyone to spend the morning with my wife without coffee"—and then he told them of his milk mistake. His colleagues thought it was hysterical, and so did I. My reaction suddenly seemed ridiculous. His gentle humor soft-

Statements to Avoid

You've heard it before, but I'll say it again. Focus on the "I feel . . ." statements, and eliminate the "you" statements. Here are some other losers to avoid.

- How can you . . .
- I don't think you want to do . . .
- You always . . .
- You never . . .
- You're so . . .
- Why can't you ever . . .
- I think you feel . . .

Which Ground Rules Work for You?

Before you begin any of the steps or negotiation points, decide what kind of environment you would like to create, and talk about or write down your ground rules for healthy discussion. Think about what does and doesn't work for both of you. Refer to them when necessary. Below are some suggestions.

- No late night, right-before-bed discussions
- No discussions in front of kids or other people
- No teasing, eye-rolling, or "tsk-ing"
- No yelling, accusing, threatening, or bullying
- No walking out on each other or emotionally checking out
- Take time to transition out of work or parenting before serious discussion
- Focus only on each other (no TV or newspaper in the background)
- Be tender with each other
- Keep your heart open

ened my anger and put it into perspective. And he did promise to never, ever use all the milk again.

INTENTIONAL STEPS
TOWARD A LOVING RELATIONSHIP

The work of marriage and parenting can be tedious, but the fruits that each bear are immeasurably rewarding. The steps that follow will help you begin your journey of defining what works for your family, your relationship, and you.

Step One: Make Your Marriage a Priority

A couple I interviewed, Jim and Louise, had not gone out alone since their children, now ages four and six, were born. "We just don't trust anyone to take care of our children," Louise explained, while her husband looked a little forlorn. Other excuses included inability to find babysitters, the expense of babysitters, or lack of extended family support. I suggested to her, a stay-at-home mother with a masters degree, that she could surely solve the problem of finding a babysitter if she wanted. "You just don't understand," she said. Jim added, "Our children are the center of our lives," but he admitted that they were neglecting themselves and their marriage.

It is easy to slip into the Couple Martyr roles, much like the Mother Martyr role. The Couple Martyr makes decisions based solely on the needs of the child and neglects their own personal and relationship needs. It's easy to get stuck in Couple Martyrdom, because we usually start in this place out of necessity: It's not Couple Martyrdom, it's just hardcore parenting, when kids are sick and work and family life are all about survival. It is when you stay fixed in the Couple Martyr position that you do damage to your relationship.

We all know well that children change our lives forever. And they change our relationships with our spouses. It gets harder, it gets better. Our love for our children intensifies our commitment to each other, yet emotional and physical intimacy diminishes over time. Without your marriage, there is no family—and children need a strong, loving family above all. There are circumstances, and even years, when it's necessary to backburner our relationships. Our children need us, and it's important to take care of urgent needs and ride out the difficult times. When these times pass—when the baby is sleeping through the night, when the transition to a new school has happened, when the workload subsides—it becomes our duty to make a good marriage one of our top priorities.

Getting married is a big commitment, but it's the easy part. Devoting yourself to having a fabulous marriage is the real work of marriage—and the truly rewarding aspect of commitment. Saying "I do" to equality, respect, emotional authenticity, honesty, compassion, and spiritual and emotional growth is what each step down the aisle should represent, one by one. Here are some techniques to help make your marriage a priority.

Talk about your life. Give each other time to talk freely about feelings, work and child-related concerns, family issues, and life. Just listen. This allows you to blow off steam you may have from other stresses in your life, such as longs days of rambunctious children or sitting in front of a computer. It's not a time to complain about or berate your spouse, but to talk about how you feel. Doing so gives your partner a glance into your interior emotional life and helps them know you intimately in that moment. Just listen, and resist the urge to "fix" any problem.

Have regular date nights. Eat sushi, see a movie, hold hands. Get out of the house and create your own couple time, even if it's just for an hour or two. When Gill and I first started date nights, we wound up getting into fights and staring angrily at each other across a table at our favorite restaurant. What a waste this seemed! But sometimes you need to have that argument you've been sweeping under the carpet in order to get to the fun stuff.

Work on it. If you have a problem, it generally will not fix itself. Get help from a counselor, minister, or other professional. One woman summed up what many couples have experienced: "We never felt like we needed counseling until we had children." I don't know anyone who cannot benefit from counseling or personal growth work, and why not? Consider it a massage or spa treatment for your psyche. The entire family reaps the benefits. Your marriage needs both regular maintenance and emergency service. Don't neglect your love and assume it will work itself out.

Choose your relationship. Marital happiness doesn't just happen; it's sustained through choice and effort. Our children will not always be happy with our choices, but as parents, it's our job to make the hard decisions for the good of the entire family—and that means sometimes choosing your relationship over the desires of the children. They might not want to be left with a babysitter. They might want to spend the day at the pool instead of helping to clean out the garage. They might feel angry that you've left them at Grandma's for a weekend getaway. Don't worry about short-term inconveniences and complaints; make choices that sustain your relationship and your family over the long haul.

I often hear men and women lamenting that their expectations for marriage must be too high, and I question what has happened to make us feel so undeserving of a loving, equal partnership. We're not afraid to have high expectations for customer service at Nordstrom, or for our children's education, or regarding behavior of professional athletes—but when it comes to our marriages we set the bar low. Some of us set it appallingly low, like the female executive with the husband who neither works nor cares for their children or the husband working 60-hour workweeks for barely a living wage, who is afraid to ask his wife to work and share the financial burden. We have every right to expect equality, ask for what we need, love our partners fiercely and deeply, and to raise the bar. The pursuit of marital happiness is a worthy and sacred calling.

Test Your Couple Martyr Behavior

There are times when your relationship must take a backseat role—a newborn baby, a sick child, financial choices, the regular commitments of having children—and you save the needs of your relationship for another day (or year!). Sacrifices can become habits, though; so knows the Couple Martyr. Test your marital mettle.

1. Do you forego spending money on yourself and only spend on your children?
2. When was the last time you had a regular social life?
3. Do you ask your children to give you time alone to talk on a daily or weekly basis?
4. Do you look down on parents who vacation alone?
5. Do you feel that leaving your children with babysitters hurts them?
6. Do you think your children are insecure or miserable without you for short periods of time?
7. Have you forgotten what you like to do together as a couple, because you only have family time together?
8. Do you find excuses not to go out together, such as expense, lack of opportunity, and the like?
9. Have you snuck off to make love lately?

Step Two: Practice Forgiveness; Allow Yourself to Be Consoled

One mother I interviewed over coffee spoke of her marriage in golden tones and then casually mentioned a "divorce folder" that she kept. Confused, I asked her what she meant, "Oh, it's a file I have that lists all the things that my husband has done wrong. Or hostile things that his mother said. That sort of thing." She then began to describe a family incident that happened over the holidays a few months back; "This went right in the divorce file, and I'm still furious at him." She had spent months holding onto her anger, withdrawing from and punishing her husband, unable to forgive him. Likewise, he had not been allowed to console her or fix the situation. They were both stuck in a horrible limbo, where she was invested in her anger, and her husband was desperately trying to console someone who was inconsolable.

We all know Alexander Pope's maxim "to err is human, to forgive divine," but why is it so hard—yet so important—for us to do this? Perhaps this is answered by another poet's words, Henry Wadsworth Longfellow: "If we could read the secret history of our enemies, we would find in each person's life sorrow and suffering enough to disarm all hostility." In other words, walking in someone else's shoes, trying to understand their pain, opens our heart and allows us to forgive them. If we have compassion for our partner's pain, we can have compassion for ourselves. Likewise, if we have compassion for ourselves, we can extend this to our partners, our children, and the world.

If you have been hurt, allow yourself to be consoled. It is a gift to both of you. Your partner is able to express love and remedy the situation. You are giving your wound or resentment a chance to heal, with your partner's words or actions as salve. Accept their apology, the tea they made for you, or the arm around your shoulders. Someday you will be administering the apology and will have great appreciation for a partner who can forgive you and receive your healing touch.

Step Three: Agree On Your Couple Culture

My mother and her husband, Bob, love all aspects of food, from leafing through seed catalogs to cooking new recipes to working weekly at the farmers' market. Their vegetable garden is an elaborate, abundant wash of flowers, vegetables, and fruit trees. Every corner has a purpose, with lemon verbena tucked here and there, rosemary delineating root vegetables from lettuce, and sunflowers and roses encircling the yard. They take great pleasure in planning their garden together and cooking or giving away the bounty, including zucchini and squashes, homemade tomato and applesauce, citrus and stone fruits, melons, and bouquets of sweet peas. Their relationship is encapsulated in their garden and the food that nourishes their family and friends.

My mother and Bob have created a couple culture defined by gardening, a deep appreciation of organic food and the Farmers' Market, and the surrounding community. Whether it involves world-class vegetable gardens, mountain biking, or playing Hearts, your couple culture is what you like to do together, what stimulates your love and your emotional and intellectual rapport. It's deciding what's important to you in your life and relationship—physical activity, arts, music, nature, friends, academics—and putting it into action.

For some, their couple culture is about creating rituals, such as weekly walks, morning cups of coffee, or date nights. As Esther, a full-time working mother of two school-age children explains, "We put our kids to bed at 8 P.M. purposely, knowing they will get up at 6:45 each morning, because it gives my husband and me a couple of hours to ourselves. Our kids have always slept in their own rooms or cribs almost since birth. This has been a tremendous decision, but one that has really helped our marriage; our kids get to bed easily and stay in bed all night. We can eat a dinner that isn't kid food; we can talk about grown-up things. We also try to go out together once a week. It's nice to be reminded, almost daily, how

Creating Couple Culture

Commit to doing something together that you love, something that doesn't involve children or a chore, or learning and experiencing something new together. Ask yourself who you want to be: What do you want to rekindle from your past, and what new interests and activities would you like to pursue? As an individual, what can you bring to your partnership?

- What live events, such as theatre, music, comedy, sports, movies, or lectures do you enjoy? How can you regularly attend these events (season tickets, once a month)?
- What physical activities, such as hiking, biking, water sports, winter sports, or dance, do you enjoy doing together? How can you build a commitment to these activities into your relationship? Playing doubles tennis every weekend, walking after work, dance class together?
- Do you have mutual hobbies that you enjoy? Antiquing, gardening, home improvement, photography, reading, scrabble, swing dancing? How can you find time to share your hobbies with each other?
- What ritual would you like to resurrect or start anew?
- Are there activities that you've always dreamt of doing together? Scuba diving, sailing, salsa dancing, political activism?

Your couple culture doesn't have to be elaborate. One of our rituals is renting a movie on Friday nights. We buy scrumptious cheeses and a baguette, toss a salad, grill steaks, and open a bottle of Côtes du Rhone. After kids go to bed, we pop in the movie and feast. It's like a date night—yet we save the cost of a babysitter and movie tickets and instead invest in great food.

lucky we are that we still enjoy being together and love each other so much."

Spending time together doing something you love can transport you from the tedium of the daily grind to a rendezvous of your hearts, minds, and bodies. Neighbors of ours, Kristy and Dan, met during a hang-gliding class, and even though they're in the throes of parenthood, they find time to hang glide together. Our good friends Andy and Emily, a busy dual-earner couple, have college basketball season tickets. Shared interests, social outings, friends, and hobbies help you grow together and remain curious about life. But this doesn't mean that you'll always have—or should have—shared activities.

Your Couple Culture should also support each other's individual interests while taking in the needs of the family. My husband loves to surf, but his surfing career is on hiatus since it takes so much time away from the family. Gill's passion for sports has changed shape to fit the family structure. He runs and competes in marathons, and I can support his long runs on the weekends. I know that supporting his own interest and hobbies is important to maintaining our individuality—and that when we then come together in partnership, we are both fulfilled, complete people. Most of the time.

Step Four: Manage Your Sleep

"If I don't get to sleep right this minute, I'm going to die," I often say. It feels that bad to be in a sleep deprivation cycle. When you think you cannot possibly get more exhausted, your child who had a cold gets an ear infection. And then your other child gets sick. And then you get sick. And the raccoons get into the garbage and

A Husband's Viewpoint

The Art of Seduction

On a recent Friday night, Karen and I pushed the limits of our wild life as parents—we ordered Chinese takeout and watched the *Antiques Road Show*. Enough was enough, though, and I grabbed the remote and shut off the TV.

"We can't do this. We never have time together, and we're just wasting it watching television." I was frowning and felt depressed. "Gill, maybe we could cuddle on the couch?" Karen suggested weakly, while yawning. She had bags under her eyes from exhaustion, as I'm sure I did. And with a 4-year-old and an infant sleeping away in the other room, I'm pretty sure her libido would have been happy to hibernate for a few years. I realized, in that moment, that desperate times called for desperate measures, so I offer up five ways that are sure to reawaken the romantic passion.

wake you up during your 1 hour of sleep. Julie, with two school-age kids, relayed a story of her appendicitis: "It was an absolute emergency procedure. I was taken to the hospital, and they said, 'We need to operate right now,' and I had no chance to prepare my kids or my husband. It was like a vacation, though! I got to lie in bed and sleep for days, drifting in and out of consciousness. My kids could only visit for a couple of hours a day, and my husband was busy shuttling them to school and all their activities. I hate to say it, but it was blissful getting all that sleep." Of course, an emergency hospital stay is not recommended as the antidote to sleep deprivation.

When we don't sleep, everything suffers. Our libido cannot possibly rise from the dead, for she's protesting suffering inflicted on the

1. Bring her *InStyle* magazine and chocolate ice cream. Soak and massage her feet, then draw a bubble bath for her. Be very, very patient. Within a month, she will begin to relax and notice you.

2. Clean the bathroom, make the bed, fold the laundry, knit her a sweater, and expect little in return. You will suddenly look very attractive.

3. Insist she go out once a week with her girlfriends while you amuse the screaming monkeys otherwise known as your children. She will come home feeling scandalous. (Note: you will be too tired and have a headache.)

4. Let her know you adore her, think she's sexy, and that you still daydream about her body. (Write her a note that reminds her of this while you're away).

5. After a day taking care of the kids, pay the bills while wearing a Speedo and army boots. Guaranteed to wake her up—in order to laugh if nothing else.

body. Clearly don't try to use your brain—to write a book for example—because your brain is not your friend when it's not rested. Basic motor skills vanish, as bruised hips attest. One woman I spoke with, who had three children ages 13, 9, and 6, said she had just started sleeping through the night in the last year. For 12 years, she didn't sleep.

Then, after not sleeping for days, months, and years, we forget how to sleep. A friend Kitty pointed out: "I lie there and my eyes hurt when I close them, because I'm so tired, but my brain has forgotten how to rest!" We're so sleep deprived, so on-call, so hyper-vigilant in attending to our children, that we don't allow ourselves to slumber like normal humans. Instead we fall into pseudosleep, ready to leap up like a crazy puppet to rush to the bedside of our children. How can

Happy Sleep, Happy Parents

The younger the children, the more exhausted the parents. Here are some tips to help you catch up on sleep.

- One or two nights a week sleeping alone, hopefully out of range of children's noise, can do wonders. Even if it's on the couch or the futon in the den.
- Cat naps. Short naps can breathe new life into wilting selves. On the weekends or before dinner, let yourself or your partner sneak down the hall and get in a little nap.
- Sleepy time at a friend's house. Jackie, mother of three, confessed that she used to go to her best friend's house to sleep. This friend didn't have noisy children roaming the halls.

we possibly thrive when a basic physical need is neglected so severely? The answer is that we don't thrive. We wilt, we get depressed, and our relationship suffers.

Our partners bear the brunt of our exhaustion. As Julie later adds, "When my kids were even smaller, I barely had enough energy to take care of them and love them, let alone be nice to my husband. Everything he did irritated me. I know I was and still am hard on him, but I can't help it. Getting from A to B is all that matters." Relationship niceties do seem more disposable than good parenting, but it's in these moments that it's even more important to be kind and loving to your partner. They can be your saviors, if you ask for their help.

Step Five: Schedule Intimacy and Romance

Before Gill and I had children, we spent time with another couple, Tim and Leilani, with young children. This couple was a riot: They joked that they had sex once a month if lucky; their most scandalous romantic fantasy involved going to a hotel room, solo, for a full night's sleep; and they said they now scheduled time for "sex dates." Certainly that's not how parenting would be for us, we joked back. Clueless as lemmings, we had no idea they were telling the truth.

The stark reality of parenting is that the personal free time we used to take for granted—the time we squandered doing who knows what!—and the free time in the relationship, is not just scaled back, it's gone. Kaput. You have an interesting life; then you have a child. Tim and Leilani, both professionals working 5 days a week, took it as an organizational challenge: They scheduled weekly relationship goals, such as "cuddle for 1 hour," or "massage time," or "talk about how to enjoy sex more," and then they would put it on the calendar. Leilani adds, "Sometimes if we made a specific sex date, we felt too much pressure. . . . 'We must have sex' felt too results-oriented—so we changed it to more about bringing us closer. If spending time talking about sex or cuddling leads to sex, then that's great, but if it doesn't, that's okay too. In the end, we're closer."

Getting out your date book or handheld computer to schedule couple time may indeed be a mood killer. For some people, leaving sex to chance might mean a few years of no-such-luck passing you by. When time has become such a precious commodity, setting goals and making intimacy dates might save our libidos from a slow death. Too frequently, we are sabotaged by all of the reasons *not* to have sex or spend time cuddling. We're too tired. We're out of shape. We can't find the Astroglide. I haven't shaved my legs. He has a 7:00 A.M. work meeting. The house is a mess. . . . The list of reasons is long and convincing, so it's good to remind yourself why sex is important.

Skin-to-skin contact reminds you that you're romantic partners. Isabella and Daniel were pretty much equal parents. Although Isabella was still nursing their youngest, Daniel was responsible for nighttime wakenings. Their workweek was divided fairly evenly, with both working about 25 hours and splitting child care in an elaborate schedule. They loved their children, they were happy with their parenting arrangement, yet Isabella confided that, "I feel like we're roommates or, worse, brother and sister. We share in loving our children, but everything is so structured that it leaves no room for spontaneity or fun or 'us'!" Daniel was feeling the lack of connection as well, so he suggested a Saturday night ritual: Sleep naked. "It's not like we have to do anything, since we're both so exhausted, but I just want to try and cuddle and enjoy each other's body in bed again."

A month later, they both reported back, independently, that the new ritual was a resounding success. Via e-mail, Isabella writes, "Feeling his warm body next to mine, with no expectations, is so sensual. Each time Saturday night rolls around, I think that there is no possible way we will have sex—because I'm exhausted or just completely uninterested. And most of the time, I get interested!" Daniel followed up with another e-mail, "Our bed feels like 'our' bed again. There's adult activity going on. We're currently considering instating a Wednesday night sleep naked ritual as well."

Sex, in all its moods, connects you. When it's done with caring, communication, love, and a little humor, sex can be poetic, wild, invigorating, freeing, sensual, or sweet. Married almost 35 years, with grown children, Pat tells of her relationship with her partner:

Let's Talk about Sex . . .

Often when I broach the topic of sex in my interviews, I'm met with silence. Perhaps there's not much to say about something we've forgotten how to do—but I suspect we still don't know how to talk about our sexuality and our sex lives. From puberty to adulthood, we're not given the vocabulary or encouraged to discuss sex with our friends or our partners. We're afraid to disclose our insecurities, our desires, and what we do or don't want.

But here's the secret: Our sexuality is what makes us human, what attracts us to our partners, inspires creativity, helps us express our love and emotions, and is a vital part of who we are. With all of these positives, it's unfortunate that we've been given so many mixed and negative messages about sexuality—resulting in sex lives that have plenty of room for improvement. Communicating with your partner is the first step toward a more complete, healthy, and exuberant sex life. Even if you're too tired or unmotivated to have sex, start talking about it.

- How has your body image evolved since you were a teenager? When have you felt strongest, most confident, sexiest?
- Does sex open the door for you to emotionally connect with your partner, or do you first need to feel emotionally connected in order to have sex?
- Have certain insecurities or sexual beliefs shaped your sexuality? Do you believe your body should look and respond a certain way or that your partner should respond a certain way?
- What do you love about your partner's body? What do you love about your partner's sexual persona?
- Imagine your sex lives now and in the future. What qualities do you want it to embody?

"Our sex life has a great history. When we got married, we were both virgins, and our sex life took off like a rocket. It was fantastic, and we felt so adventurous and lucky, as if we had discovered a secret world known only to us. When we had children, we definitely had a slump.

Tools of the Trade

After having my first baby and still carrying an extra 30 pounds or so, I invoked a sex rule: Nighttime only and lights out! It was hard enough reconnecting with my sexuality and partner without sunlight or bedroom lamps spotlighting my roly-poly belly and stretch marks. I needed to make it as comfortable and romantic as possible for myself, taking all of my new emotional needs and insecurities into account. (I would have time to overcome those later, I hoped.)

Every day we are given little messages, which stick like gum on a shoe. The best love and romance is spontaneous. Hot and heavy passion is lurking around every corner. And that the kitchen table is actually a comfortable, exciting place to have sex. Well, parents know better. It takes planning and preparation, tenderness and a mattress, to help romance lift off. And, please, don't forget the lubricant.

Stock the supplies you need and consider the mood you want to create for your next sex date. It's not a mood-enhancer when you cannot find the matches for candlelight in the middle of a tryst—and you start arguing over who didn't put them back in the kitchen drawer. So, plan and prepare. Here are some ideas.

- The supplies—lubricant, birth control, fancy oils, creams, or love potions
- Candles, matches
- Music (an album, CD, or tape—not a radio station with ads)
- Location, location, location. Is it private, cozy, safe? Child- and pet-free?

Like a 20-year slump! During that time, sex helped us reconnect and express ourselves physically when maybe the words were not there. It wasn't fireworks, but it was tender and loving. When our third, and last, child went off to college, the empty nest was a sexual wake-up call. Our sexuality had been pretty dormant. Now we've entered a whole new phase. We're so together, in all ways, that sex feels very pure now, sometimes wild and kinky, and other times we end up laughing hysterically because of a hip cramp."

Working through sexual challenges brings you closer. It's hard to make yourself completely vulnerable, which is what sex asks you to do. Especially with children down the hall, especially when your body is not your own and when life—and your relationship—has become so complicated. If your sex life has always been a struggle, life-with-children surely doesn't help. Use the exercises included, or invest time with a counselor who can help you overcome issues that may be blocking you from having a rich, passionate, soulful sex life. A deeper understanding of your partner's sexuality, and vice versa, creates emotional intimacy and safety, which can lead to greater physical intimacy.

Final Step: Create Your Relationship Goals

Now that you've discussed, discovered, and prioritized what's important in your relationship, it helps to detail specific actions that will support your hearts' intention. Use the chart below to help you and your partner examine, explore, establish, and enact ways to improve and sustain your relationship.

The major area of priority should be written in the Examine column. For each area, list the aspects of that priority you'd like to discuss in the Explore column. Notice we're not jumping to solutions quite yet—it's better (and less threatening) at first to agree to explore what is going on and generate some ideas on how to address them. Give your spouse a chance to openly discuss this, and you may be surprised at the insights and different perspectives he has on your relationship. Once you've done that, decide together what you need to do to recharge your relationship, and put that in the Establish column. Finally, agree to the specific measures to bring your relationship goals to fruition. Enter these measurable actions in the Enact column.

A completed chart might look like this.

Examine	Explore	Establish	
Communication	Talk about your life. Understand your anger patterns. Get outside help if you need tune-up.	Daily and weekly ritual. Read this section together; how do you show anger to your partner? Talk with counselor or other professional.	
Time together	How can you make time for you as a couple?	Date night, weekend get-away, Tuesdays at restaurant, Friday movie night at home.	
Romance and intimacy	What element is our marriage missing?	Fulfill need for physical intimacy. Express your love. Commit to healthy sex discussions. Get tools of the trade.	
Couple culture	What is important to your family?	Live events (theatre, music, sports). Physical activities. Hobbies. Rituals. Learning something new.	
Managing your sleep	How do we resolve this when we get in "sleep trouble?" What are each person's sleep needs?	Sleep in separate rooms once in a while.	

NEGOTIATION POINTS

These negotiation points are more about defining terms in your relationship: What does romance mean to you? How do you express your love? How do you share and fulfill dreams? A date night may seem like a relationship balm, but it's the content of the date—the conversation, the intent, the meaning behind your words and gestures—that makes a potentially routine date night feel intimate and special.

Enact

Stay up one night each week after kids are in bed to talk about family, home. Have a code word or phrase that can let your partner know you are angry or upset; break the anger pattern. Who will schedule appointment? Will you go together?

Who can provide child care? Grandparents? Close friends? Babysitter?

Sleep naked every Saturday night. Write love notes; make casual physical contact a part of your day; hold hands, give hugs. Use books, magazine articles to initiate discussion. Go shopping together: What do you need? What looks like fun?

Buy tickets; have seasonal subscriptions. Join a gym together; take advantage of onsite child care. Start a collection; join a couples-only book club. Cook dinner together once a week; discuss politics, work, education. Sign up for class at local YMCA.

Split weekend early-morning duties; let one person sleep in while the other starts the day with the family.

Likewise, it's the negotiated dreams and shared values that make your life meaningful and real. As a woman married 23 years described, "Fred always wanted to go homestead on a mountaintop in Alaska; I could never bear the isolation. So we lived on 10 acres in a rural, wooded area when I would have liked to be closer to shopping malls. I longed to live for a while in a Spanish-speaking country to become totally fluent in the language, so he researched what it would take to obtain residency in Costa Rica. To that end, we just started a tropical hardwood plantation there, and he has started learning Spanish—from his enthusiasm, people can no longer tell whose dream it originally was. In fact, we sometimes forget! (He named the business after me—now that's romantic!)"

Looking at the issues below, share, learn about your partner, and negotiate your romance. Let go of what you *think* the other should want; just because you like to give your wife chocolates and flowers doesn't mean she isn't fantasizing about the latest literary fiction or a lovely rose-scented body lotion. For some, a romantic date might be a fancy dinner, and for others, it's a tennis match. Sexy might be defined as going to bed in a t-shirt and underwear, in the buff, or head to toe in silk and lace. When it comes to negotiating love issues, dive right in and try to deeply know the other. And take it lightly: Don't squash romance by putting your demands on the table. This is a chance to find out how to love your partner in the way they need to be loved and to have it reciprocated in the unique way in which you need to be loved.

Romance Definitions

How do you like to express romance?

What makes you feel cherished?

What activities feel meaningful?

What speaks to your senses (music, food, outdoor activities, other)?

Define terms of endearment

What is sexy to you? At bedtime, all the time, smells, tastes, music . . .

Communication

Define best circumstances to talk about "issues"

How often?

"Emergency" situations

When to call on counseling

How to have a couple "time-out"

How will you reconnect?

Gift-Giving Philosophy

Gifts with meaning (special items, time, experiences)

Holidays, birthdays, anniversaries

Spending ideals

Cards

Spontaneity

Personal Needs

Exercising

Time alone

Spiritual/meditative practice

Time with friends

Couple Vision

Common dreams

Health and physical goals

Vacation philosophy

INTENTION: COMMIT TO A STRONG, HAPPY RELATIONSHIP BASED ON EQUALITY

We are able to love and support each other best when each person's role is valued equally, and our respective roles have been negotiated and agreed upon. Equal doesn't mean sharing everything 50/50. That would be impossible and impractical, as Cinda, a mother of two teenagers explained: "People are better at different things, and in a successful relationship, you have to foster and support the differences that you and your partner bring to the table. I'm not sure having everything totally equal works for every relationship. It is only when the power or workload is tipped in one direction that it's detrimental. Substantial power over someone else's life is never appropriate in relationships, and neither are substantial work burdens." Another mother adds, "Living life and raising children is not like measuring out grains of rice. Each of you has strengths that you bring to the table—why not use those? I hate unloading the dishwasher, but don't mind doing dishes or loading. I think it's more important to find a good mix to show your kids how each of us is unique and can be very good at one thing and not so good at another. And you know what? That's okay. Not everyone is going to be a pianist, and not everyone is going to be an accountant."

Valuing each other's role equally and treating the responsibility of parenting as an equal partnership underlines the seriousness with which you support each other: As primary parent or coparent, your concerns and needs are listened to, and as provider or coprovider, your pressures and needs are acknowledged. As full-time working mom Hannah describes, "I think Scott and I both really appreciate the other person's support, because we have both experienced the stay-at-home parent role, at different times, due to job switching. We treat each other with respect and try to be on the same team." Valuing each other, respecting each other, loving each other. These are the true ideals of marriage.

Loving Each Other Intention Statement:

We commit to an emotionally healthy relationship based on valuing and respecting each other.

_____   _____
           Signed   Signed

CHAPTER 4

Managing Work and Money

"Certainly, countless couples do both work,
and both share the child care as much as they can
and work hard to find some sort of balance in their lives.
It's just that the 'balance' is usually structured around
a bottom line that the woman's life is the source
of flexibility and the man's job cannot be touched."

–Naomi Wolf, *Misconceptions*

Maria practically sprinted through the doors of the restaurant, quickly rushing to my table, "I'm so sorry I'm late," she said. She was stylishly groomed—with an energy level that suggested a caffeine drip. Her cell phone ringing, she apologized, "I have to keep it on for the babysitter." Like many moms who work full-time, Maria felt chronically late for everything, always on call, and required to keep an energy level high enough to accomplish the jobs of two people—mother and employee. On top of this, she had just gotten a promotion for a job she had coveted for years, IT manager at a shipping company: "It's a mixed blessing, of course. I just missed Halloween with my kids, because we had a technical emergency. So while I was exhilarated to take care of the emergency for my company, I felt guilty about missing Halloween."

Maria loves her job, and she shares with me that she is the high earner in her family—a growing reality in today's family, with 30 percent of couples reporting the wife as the high wage earner. Maria beams with pride as she explains that she and her husband are able to send their two kids to an elite private school. When I ask Maria about her choice to work full-time, she looks exasperated. "You sound just like my mother! 'It's your choice to work so much! You're neglecting your children,' she says. But why is it my choice? I want what's best for my children, and that includes a secure financial situation where I can give them the best education and live in a decent neighborhood. Why is it that nobody asks my husband how come he's choosing to work full-time? I tell you, it infuriates me."

As Maria's story illustrates, the mere idea of a "woman's choice" places an unfair burden on a woman: It seems that we alone must choose—between a job that provides financial security or personal fulfillment and providing at-home care for our children. This "choice" is even more loaded when you throw in lack of part-time work options, inadequate child care, and financial needs. Ann Crittenden, in *The Price of Motherhood,* points out, "The big problem with the rhetoric of choice is that it leaves out power. Those who benefit from the status quo always attribute inequities to the choices of the underdog. The current rhetoric about choosing motherhood sounds suspiciously like the 1950s rhetoric about 'happy' women. . . . But mothers' choices are not made in a vacuum. They are made in a world that women never made, according to rules they didn't write."

We hear the rhetoric of choice from many sources—academic studies, news stories, social trends, and talk shows. The "right choice" depends on the messenger and audience. If you work to make ends meet, you're the victim of inadequate child care options. If you pursue an aggressive career path, you're cast as selfish, with warped priorities. If you don't work, you're squandering your talent and productivity. Some choice-related arguments even suggest that most mothers working *really* don't have to work—families are just mismanaging their finances. Finally, if we work for a better lifestyle, we're materialistic and greedy. Appallingly, these arguments are applied exclusively to the choices of mothers, completely leaving fathers out of the equation. Critics are kindhearted and sympathetic to fathers who get promotions and increased job responsibilities or make money to elevate family status and security—even if it means they must travel more and work longer hours. The message is ironic: Women should make family a priority by minimizing their working selves, and men should make family a priority by working harder to provide a better lifestyle.

On the upside, this argument for choice can release women from jobs or careers they dislike. Although it's not easy to start over or incur financial setbacks for doing so, many women report more personal work fulfillment as they reinvent their working selves and find their niche. Lucy, a former corporate manager who now runs financial workshops for women, explained, "My children inspired me to choose my work carefully and be creative about my options." It is no surprise that woman-owned small businesses are ubiquitous, as are part-time or freelance woman independent contractors, nurses, designers, counselors, teachers, administrative assistants, and more. (It is also these part-time mothers who are volunteering in schools and libraries across the country, augmenting our children's education with their unpaid labor.)

The lack of choice for men can be just as significant, handcuffing

The Career and Finances Quiz

It's impossible—and unnecessary—to compare the love of our children with pursuing one's mission in life. The two are intertwined. Love, constant and unwavering, must be translated into action, into being physically present for our children, but it's not exclusive to loving ourselves and pursuing our own path. We owe this to our children, providing a model of a fulfilled, engaged, resourceful adult. We owe this to ourselves, through all our ages and stages. How are you doing?

1. Do you describe your work as a career or a job?
2. How important is your work to your identity? Can you imagine life without work?
3. Have you ever had trouble combining work and family? Do you feel that it's easier or harder for your partner?
4. Do you feel at peace with work sacrifices you may have made?
5. Do you think your partner has made like sacrifices and is at peace?

them to their traditional role. Seth, a father of two children and businessman who has chosen to work a part-time schedule in order to equal parent with his wife, says, "I get very frustrated, because men don't see that they have a choice. We are disadvantaged, because it's not socially acceptable for us to choose from the full range of choices that women have available. But men are weak, because they don't see they have a choice nor do they have the courage to take a different path. It's lack of awareness. It's fear about losing social status. For most of us, work and a paycheck still define self-worth." Seth is adamant about being formally involved in parenting his children, and he has experienced resistance from his wife. "She thought money was the symbol of my love for the family, not time I spent with them. She came from

6. Close your eyes and take three deep breaths—and describe in two sentences how you do or don't maintain balance in you life.

7. How many times has a work-related meeting been interrupted by a child or a call from the babysitter?

8. When was the last time your children came to work with you?

9. Do you know the cost of day care or preschool, your babysitters, ballet lessons or Pee Wee football?

10. What is your checkbook balance? Your estimated taxes? The interest rate on your home mortgage or auto loan?

11. What are the exact locations of these three documents in your home: taxes for last year, birth certificates for your children, and a copy of your rental or home property insurance?

12. List the last two occasions about which you spoke to your health insurance company.

13. Who managed filing your taxes for the past few years?

a very traditional background, so it's taken her a while to see the value of me as an involved and participatory father, believe it or not."

Regardless of your choice, your decisions about work are nobody's business but your own. The expression, "motherhood is the most important job in the world," needs a facelift: *Parenting* is the most important job in the world. It should be implicit that it's not necessary for women alone to sacrifice earning power while their partners remain single-mindedly focused on a paycheck or career track. As anthropologist Sarah Blaffer Hrdy sums up: "A woman's career ambition is not a thing apart from her nurturing, maternal feelings, or an expression of vestigial 'masculinity,' or the delusional product of contemporary feminism, as some have suggested. Instead, ambitiousness

Quick Tips

If your work or finance discussions end up in intense disagreements, here are five things in this chapter that might have the most immediate impact.

1. With your partner, take time to do the "How Do You Feel about Work" section on page 117.
2. Discuss the challenges of working full-time or part-time and parenting full-time—and then discuss the benefits of the different roles.
3. Each write down your fears around work.
4. Have a session talking about your career goals. If you're the listener, ask questions, be curious, and listen.
5. Establish your financial commandments using the exercise at end of the chapter (see "Our Financial Commandments" on page 145).

can be a reflection of the fact that, among many species, the more powerful and politically dominant the individual, the greater is her or his reproductive success."

In order to approach parenting as equal partners, men must find sidelining careers compelling as well as socially permissible. As Rhona Mahony says in *Kidding Ourselves*, "Obviously, the real challenge is to attract large numbers of men into shifting from full-time work to part-time work. What will make men willing to risk conflict and stigma at work by requesting part-time work? They will do it when their wives make it a condition of fatherhood and have the bargaining power to back up the proposal." Until men and women are encouraged to share equally in parenting choices, we will continue to perpetuate a society that gives lip service to valuing women—but not men—for "giving it all up" for the children.

WHAT WORKS ABOUT WORK FOR WOMEN

"The childrearing years correspond precisely to the time when many women's careers are coming together—and these careers represent a lifetime of effort. For them, giving up work would amount to nothing less than being stripped of an integral part of their selfhood."

—Judith Warner, *Working Mother*
magazine

You're damned if you do, damned if you don't. But one thing is for certain: Few things spur passionate debate and emotions more than working mothers. According to a recent Census Bureau publication, 55 percent of women with infants were in the labor force in June 2000, compared with 31 percent in 1976. And the older your children get, the more likely you are working: For mothers with children over a year, 73 percent worked in 1998, with 52 percent working full-time. More women are graduating from college and business school than men, and women are obtaining advanced degrees overall in almost equal numbers to men. Women are financially contributing in measurable ways like never before. Clearly, career goals and the idea of fulfilling, challenging, or financially rewarding work is a vital part of what defines women today.

Ellen Galinsky, president of the Families and Work Institute, explained in an article in the *New York Times*, "I still meet people all the time who believe that the trend has turned, that more women are staying home with their kids, that there are going to be fewer dual-income families, but it's just not true." In fact, a Virginia Slims poll in 1998 found that only 7 percent of mothers who work claim that they'd rather be full-time, stay-at-home moms. No doubt, women in the workplace are no trend; they're here to stay. So what does this say about working mothers? Women are working:

❊ To financially support and contribute to their families

❊ Because paid work ensures that they're building financial security by contributing to social security and 401(k)s and developing their own credit history

❊ Because outside work gives them more equality in their marriage

❊ For mental stimulation and challenge

❊ Because paid work gives them confidence and feelings of self-sufficiency

❊ For social interaction and exchange with others

❊ Because they want to model a working mother for their children

❊ To provide a better quality of life for their family

In other words, women work for many of the same reasons that men work—they like it, they have to, they need the money, they need stimulation, they need the escape. Marilyn Yalom surmises in *A History of the Wife*, "There are several reasons why married women like to work. In the first place, they do not want to be economically dependent on their husbands. . . . A second, and in my opinion equally important, reason why married women choose to work is that they do not want to be confined to the perimeters of the home. They do not want to operate within the cagelike frame of traditional domesticity. Greater education for women has meant that their horizons extend far beyond the kitchen, the parlor, and the garden."

Work is even good for women's health: Rosalind Barnett and Caryl Rivers report in *She Works/He Works*, "A federally funded study of 745 married women shows working women to be in better emotional health than those who are not employed," and a survey of depression in 1,000 families, taken in 1990, found that nonworking, stay-at-home mothers were among the most severely depressed.

Just as for men, there are compromises with work. Women take the job with less travel, miss a promotion, or cut down hours to be available to their children. For our children and our families, there are consequences to our working: We miss a softball game, cannot volunteer to run the school play, and aren't always home for dinner. As Peggy Orenstein found in her engaging book, *Flux*, "The working

How Do You Feel about Work?

We all have different relationships with work. For some of us it's a means to an end. We work hard so that we can get home at the end of the day or so we can one day retire. Some of us thrive in the workplace. We find great satisfaction in managing a doctor's office or creating a perfect spreadsheet. Most likely your feelings about work stem from your parents' work ethic and jobs—and whether you've stumbled upon, or worked toward, a job or career you love. It's unlikely that a couple will see eye-to-eye on work. In my marriage I see work as part of my mission in life, and my husband sees it as drudgery. This can be a great source of misunderstanding if you haven't explored your feelings together.

- Were your parents happy or proud of their work?
- Was there any family or community stigma if your mother worked?
- Growing up, did you work in your neighborhood or community?
- How did you feel when you first began earning money?
- What do you like and dislike about working?
- Have you ever had a job you loved?
- How important is your work to your sense of self-worth and identify?
- Do you think of work as drudgery, something you must do, or as your mission in life?

mothers sometimes felt regret or guilt over missing small, irretrievable moments of their children's lives; often they pondered the meaning of success and power; but self-worth was not at issue. In fact, they often felt like excellent role models, especially for their daughters." In the end, work offers a complex array of possibilities for both women and men, yet problem-solving the challenges of work and family balance is still primarily the domain of mothers.

HOW ARE WE STRUGGLING?

Nobody has it easy, that much is clear, whether doing full-time paid work outside the home or stay-at-home parenting managing house and children. The balancing act is a constant struggle, as are the doubts we have and questions we pose to ourselves about what's best for our families, finances, identities, and, of course, our children.

Profile of a Full-Time Working Mother

Daphne is a powerhouse venture capitalist. An animated woman who is quick to laugh, she clearly likes to be in charge, with no apologies. Daphne and her husband, Andrew, both work full-time, demanding jobs, although she describes her job as higher stress. The mother of a 5-year-old, Daphne describes her ideal scenario for motherhood before having her daughter: "I definitely wanted to keep working and do the supermom thing—the work all day, come home, make dinner, perfect wife thing. I didn't have any clear kind of vision what it was truly going to be like, and I certainly had no role models to emulate." Daphne's updated version of a supermom was to work in a highly competitive and financially rewarding environment and make cookies at midnight for the class party the next day.

She describes her beginning years as a parent: "I was pretty happy to go back to work after taking 6 months off to be with my daughter. The big lesson I learned is that I wasn't cut out to be a full-time mom. I would go bonkers if I ever tried to do that. Working is definitely easier. Oh, my God, I had no idea how much easier it was! Staying home rocked me to the core." Daphne's sentiments echo what has become, for many, the new mother confession: I'd go nuts if I stayed home all day. Yet she feels conflicted, judges her own competence as a parent, and has decided not to have another child: "On an average day, I feel like I'm not there for anybody and that I haven't done anything right. And to add another child into that? There's no way. Although I'd like for my daughter to have a sibling, the price is too high on my career and marriage. I can barely devote enough time to my one child as it is." Daphne is part of a new phenomenon of women who choose to have one-child families because they believe their marriages and careers cannot withstand the demands on time and responsibility that come with a second child—and they believe it's not fair to a second child.

The choice to have fewer children in hopes of a better quality of life is nothing new, says Sarah Blaffer Hrdy, "Mothers have worked for as long as our species has existed, and they have depended on others to help them rear their children." She also points out, "Wherever women have both control over their reproductive opportunities and a chance to better themselves, women opt for well-being and economic security over having more children."

Daphne lists the personal struggles she has gone through since becoming a mom. Lack of personal time. Body image issues. Reliving past, dark experiences from her childhood. A marriage that suffers. "Guilt is huge with me. No matter where I land, I always think about the thing I'm not doing, which takes up so much energy." When asked if she believes her husband spends time feeling guilty about his parenting choices, she responds, "Not a chance. But that's not a bad thing. I don't find any particular satisfaction in being the one to feel guilty. It's not healthy, and I know that. I just can't help it." She concludes that she loves her work: "It's part of who I am, through and through," and she feels that, despite the guilt, she never regrets working full-time.

As a full-time working mother and family breadwinner, Dianne Lake sums up her experience in an article in *Salon* magazine: "At least, one might reason, the breadwinner mom doesn't have to do the laundry. Well, I am here to tell you that domestic chores have resisted any revolutionary change. I know only one breadwinner mom who goes to the office each day knowing that her husband will scrub the toilet and shop for food. . . . Do my husband and I wish we could trade places? Sure. Chastened by the backbreaking work of caring for children, stay-at-home dads often are eager to resume their careers or begin new ones. Breadwinner moms, me included, miss our kids a lot and long for a turn at the stay-at-home parent—at least until the laundry pile is high and the diaper supply is low. Then, we privately admit, going to the office might not be such a bad gig after all."

Questions for Couples about Full-Time Work

- What are the benefits to working full time? The frustrations?
- How have you supported, or not supported, each other's full-time work schedule throughout your children's lives?
- Are various stages in your children's lives more conducive to working full-time for either spouse?
- What judgments do you have about full-time working parents, including your own self-criticism?

Profiles of Part-Time Working Mothers

As many part-time working moms will tell you, they feel like they have the best—and worst—of both worlds. They are stimulated by their work environment, enjoy the satisfaction that comes from earning a paycheck, and covet the time they have with their children. Yet there are significant costs to working part-time—and women are most vulnerable. "Since women typically are responsible for . . . child- and elder care, it is not surprising that they account for approximately two-thirds of the part-time workforce. . . . Unfortunately, choosing part-time employment comes at a considerable cost for these workers, primarily in the form of lower wages, lack of health and pension benefits, diminished opportunities for advancement, and limited access to higher-wage industries," writes Jeffrey Wenger in an article for the Economic Policy Institute. Although the flexibility that comes with a 30-hour workweek can be ideal for many working parents, many complain that they're not taken seriously at their jobs.

As the primary parent, often with a partner working long hours, the management of the children and household can be overwhelming. "'A lot of women reduce their work hours to have more time with their children or partner,' says Rosalind Barnett. 'But if they're spending the extra time on household tasks, that doesn't translate into better relationships with their family, whether it's the spouse or the children.'"

Stacy, mother of two and marketing consultant, describes it as ". . . straddling two worlds. One minute I'm in my suit driving like a bat out of hell to a meeting, reviewing my pitch in my head for a presentation to a potential client. The next minute I'm talking with another mom about volunteering for some event at my kid's school. Sometimes it's win-win, but often it's lose-lose. I feel like the clients don't respect my availability boundaries, and my husband doesn't respect my work time. I'm either rushing to meet a deadline or rushing to take my daughter to gymnastics or rushing to my therapist to help me work on not rushing so much," she jokes. But she wouldn't trade being part of both worlds—the worlds of work and parenting—for anything.

One woman I met with, Margery, is a part-time teacher at an elementary school. Her husband, a full-time student, spends as much time studying and researching as she does teaching, so the time each spend out of the home is more or less equal. Margery explains, "I think the parenting has been equitable up until now because Juan has been available—and he hasn't been making very much money at all. I think it will continue even when he becomes a professor, because Juan now has such a solid relationship with our daughter. And he loves being a father. He's really good at it. Yeah, he doesn't do all the stuff that I think he should do, like taking care of the house and her room and the boring stuff. But he's really good at being with her and giving himself over completely to her. But I'm still 'in charge' of everything. At least in my mind. I think that for women, however much we work or not, we take responsibility for all of it."

Another part-time worker, Alma, came to an interview session having just left her second child, a 12-week old baby, at home alone for the first time with her husband. She was clearly thrilled to be out with a group of women, speaking with verve about parenting and gender roles. A former full-time worker logging in about 50 to 55 hours a week, she had cut down to 30 hours a week after the birth of her first child, now 4 years old. Alma gave us the nutshell version of her life: "Before we had kids, my husband used to joke that I was the main breadwinner. Working came easy to me; I was good at it, and I love being productive and interacting with people. But when we had our first child, it was just assumed that I would be the one to cut back at my job. There was no discussion around it, and I just accepted it as what I was supposed to do.

Now, with two children, I feel even more of a pull to work less. My 30 hours often turns into 35 or 40, plus a commute, and it just feels wrong that we're both away from our kids so much of the time."

When asked about the importance that she and her spouse attribute to their jobs and working identities, Alma responded, "I love working, but I also have my children's interests in mind. My husband, on the other hand, loves to work, period. It's his passion, and it's about the only thing he really does, besides spend time with us. So, I guess I feel more obligated to pull back in my job and be home with kids, because I care more about other things." Women who had taken maternity leaves and been able to spend time with their children were often more willing to alter their career paths and pull back on their jobs. Similarly, men who take paternity leaves or have unexpected periods of unemployment during their children's younger years bond more closely to their children—and this bond colors most of their future work decisions, often resulting in a desire to work less.

Most part-time moms seem to be highly motivated to work in order to financially contribute to their families and also to maintain a link to their working selves. They have willingly adapted their jobs or sidelined careers in order to spend time with their children while running their households, but there is often a lingering resentment toward their partners as they handle stressful work environments and most of the family maintenance. Since the average workweek in the United States is now 49 hours, a substantial difference from the 40-hour average worked in the 1950s, it seems that the breadwinner who is "Working Nine to Five . . ." is an extinct species—and that a 35-hour workweek is now labeled part-time and arranged around similar hours that the nine-to-five worker used to log.

Working Mother magazine recently found that most women continue to work, even while desiring to work less: "Many dream of 20-

Questions for Couples on Working Part-Time

- What have been the challenges of working part-time? The advantages?
- Does a part-time schedule appeal to either of you?
- How can you protect the part-time worker in your family, if necessary, with benefits?
- If one of you is working part-time and the other full-time, do you sense an imbalance in the work and family load?

to 30-hour-a-week schedules or of working from home. But what they emphatically do not wish to do is stop working, they say. It isn't that they don't love their kids. It's just that, without work, their lives wouldn't be, well, livable."

A cautionary note: Women who work part-time face stresses in their marriages that women who work full-time may not. Managing part-time work and the majority of the child and house-related responsibilities indicates an imbalance in some marriages—and an ensuing struggle often occurs. "In a survey of nearly 100 women physicians in two-career couples with at least one child under 14, those who worked full-time reported better relationships with their husbands than those working reduced hours. Marital quality may actually suffer when mothers work part-time," Barnett says.

Profiles of Stay-at-Home Mothers

Women who are able and choose to stay home say they cherish the time with their children. But as the full- and part-time working moms above show, there is no perfect prescription for every stay-at-home parent. Jeanette Lisefski, founder of the National Organization of At-

Home Mothers (www.athomemothers.com) sensitively writes on their Web site about the issues that stay-at-home mothers face: "Our need to feel appreciated by our family and/or society. . . . Our need to build our self-esteem and identity." Interestingly, in an article on the same Web site, Suzanna Mullenneaux gives this description: "At-home mothering in our time is a very demanding and complex profession that requires strength, determination, and flexibility. The at-home mother of today is often a dynamic, multifaceted professional who is not only caring wholeheartedly for the needs of her children but also pursuing her own interests, possibly earning an income from home, and taking care of herself physically and emotionally." Ironically, for an organization aiming to support stay-at-home mothers, they offer information about how to start you own business and make money from home.

Today's stay-at-home mothers, according to the United States Census Bureau, are not necessarily from high-income families. Money isn't the determining factor, as a support organization, Stay at Home Mom (SAHM) highlights: "Mothers at home today have specifically chosen to devote their time and energy toward raising a family. This is a benefit over moms of the 1950s through 1970s, who felt that staying home was their only option. Modern SAHMs have the opportunity to serve as role models and to show others that motherhood is a compelling, honorable, and very important career choice."

Phyllis, a former practicing lawyer, spent an evening with me and a few other women discussing her feelings about leaving her job to raise her children and take care of her spouse. A mother of two children, Phyllis describes her situation, "Financially, I'm lucky enough not to have to work. I like to work, and I will probably go back when my youngest starts first grade, but my work is not totally fulfilling to me, which is why I don't mind not working. I don't handle the stress well at all. I'm just not a good mother under those circumstances." After a high-stress job in a law firm, suffering insomnia before depositions and brief deadlines, Phyllis is pleased—on many levels—to stay home. "Right now, I love puttering around the house. I like doing housework. I do e-mail on the computer to keep in touch with friends and colleagues. Every day I wake up and think it's great that I don't have to put on a business suit and sit in an office missing my children. I can just take the kids to the mall, or in the summertime we can go swimming every day. I'm with my children, and I love it."

Yet, in the same conversation, I notice Phyllis making comments under her breath about "how her husband doesn't value her role as homemaker, how he doesn't contribute to running the household at all," and how she herself is embarrassed to say "full-time mom" when asked about employment. She chalks it up to her own problem with self-esteem—"it's just an identity problem. I liked work and my professional self, but I have to get over that." Phyllis examines her conflicting feelings by asking a series of questions, "My concern is, why are we in a culture where we as women feel like we're sacrificing our careers and ourselves in order to be stay-at-home moms? Why have we created a culture in which a stay-at-home mom is somehow not valued?" As we try to navigate these contradictions, the larger question becomes illuminated: Does the self-esteem of stay-at-home moms plummet because they stay home with children and aren't involved in paid labor or meaningful outside work, or because the role of mother and housewife isn't valued in our society? (And, of course, what about the value of fathers staying home?)

Later, Phyllis expresses gratitude to her husband for "allowing" her to stay home, reluctantly acknowledging her contribution to the family and to the building of his career. "I guess that I don't value the homemaker role. I feel so grateful to my husband for letting me stay home. Intellectually, I know my contribution is of equal value, but the other thing is, really, that my husband is a loving parent." As for what Phyllis feels her husband appreciates about her role? "Oh, my husband definitely does value my role. I mean, if only because his career is so important to him, and when I am working it interferes with his career. It really does. Because if somebody is sick, then he might have to stay home or he might have to pick up Julia at day care by 6:00. And that's a problem for him. It allows him to pursue his goals and gives him peace of mind knowing I'm taking care of the kids." Phyllis ends the interview reaffirming that she loves being a stay-at-home mother and feels lucky to be able to choose to do so—and she admits that it isn't all a rosy picture, but that she's chosen what's best for their family.

Patricia, a former full-time working woman, has chosen a similar path as Phyllis, leaving a high-stress job to stay-at-home parent while her husband works full-time. Unlike Phyllis, Patricia left a job she loved. Her decision to stop working also meant downsizing their family's lifestyle, including moving and buying a smaller home. "There are things I really love about being home," Patricia says, although she also admits to feeling unfulfilled; she is currently contemplating having another child to see if having three children will fill her "void," as she calls it. "I don't feel like I've truly experienced motherhood, and I'm trying to embrace it totally," she says, although her children are now both in school. "I haven't let go of the ideal of working. I had such attachment to my working self, but now I find myself at a place where I can let that go. I think I can," she says unconvincingly

Patricia explains that her work gave her a sense of personal fulfillment and accomplishment and reluctantly considers that this could be the "void" that she is feeling. She doesn't consider working part-time: "My mother really resented the fact that she had to work. It was real psychic punishment, so I want to be a stay-at-home parent and not have work as something that comes between me and my parenting."

Whether she has given up a meaningful career or a job she never particularly liked, every woman has her own idea of what being a stay-at-home mom represents. Joannie, a part-time massage therapist and mother of two school-age children, describes the contradiction perfectly: "I would love to be able to stay at home and not have to worry about work. I was raised to believe that stay-at-home moms are the be-all and end-all, probably because my father died when I was young,

Questions for Couples on Stay-at-Home Parenting

- What does being a stay-at-home parent mean to you?
- If you are the stay-at-home parent, would you consider trading roles with your partner?
- What are the joys of staying at home with children? What are the struggles?
- Do you feel there are social judgments or expectations about staying at home to parent?

and my mother worked very hard to take care of us financially. Yet even though I love the idea of staying home and devoting myself to my family, the idea of being self-sufficient is important to me. I do enjoy my work, too. I'm not sure what the perfect mothering scenario really is—or if one even exists."

THE EQUAL PARENTING AGREEMENT TO BALANCE WORK AND MONEY

We commit to equally valuing each other's working life and sharing responsibility for decision-making related to work and family finances.

Managing our working lives and money certainly makes the top-10 list of difficult challenges for parents. Our childhoods and adult experiences intertwine to inform our current choices and decisions. The goal of this chapter and EPA section is to help you understand the power you have to make decisions that support your family and your own personal growth. You're not emulating the television role models of June and Ward Cleaver: These imaginary characters misrepresented reality for most families, yet were held up as a symbol of the all-American family. It's as if someone took *Mr. Roger's Neighborhood* and said 'Now, all neighborhoods must be rubberstamped to be the same.' Sounds outrageous, doesn't it? Eddie Murphy certainly made it seem so in his *Saturday Night Live* parody, "Mr. Robinson's Neighborhood." So, sketch your own family portrait, with working lives, kids, and neighborhoods that represent you and your community.

Before you Begin: Understanding the Unencumbered Worker Model

There is a reason that we're having trouble balancing our lives—and why most of corporate America would be happy if we went back to the stay-at-home parent/breadwinner model. It's called the unencumbered worker. As explained in a publication from the Economic Policy Institute, "An unencumbered worker is an employee who behaves in the workplace as if he or she has a wife at home full-time, performing all of the unpaid care work that families require. . . . The expectation is that personal problems will not be brought into the workplace and that conflicting demands will be resolved in favor of the requirements of the job." Yet with most parents working, there is not a stay-at-home parent to manage the myriad household tasks and take care of the child-related needs seamlessly. Kathleen Christenson has dubbed this "the new mathematics of the family," according to an Economic Policy Institute article. In a dual-earner family, there are actually three jobs—two wage earners and a household manager—two paid and one unpaid. This explains why two parents often feel as if they never have enough time to get everything done—because, in fact, they don't.

In her book, *Unbending Gender*, academic Joan Williams explains the three assumptions that keep our current gender system, what she calls "domesticity," in place: the entitlement of employers to hire ideal or unencumbered workers; for men to be those unencumbered workers; and "for children to have mothers whose lives are framed around caregiving." Equal parenting asks that you start with the simple act of beginning to understand and question these roles in your families. The end goal should be intentionally creating a world which releases both men and women from traditional roles so that they may be *truly* unencum-

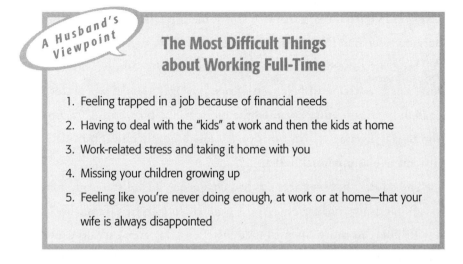

A Husband's Viewpoint

The Most Difficult Things about Working Full-Time

1. Feeling trapped in a job because of financial needs

2. Having to deal with the "kids" at work and then the kids at home

3. Work-related stress and taking it home with you

4. Missing your children growing up

5. Feeling like you're never doing enough, at work or at home—that your wife is always disappointed

bered and choose the roles that best suit them and their family, unfettered by social pressures, expectations, or assumptions. We can then join hands and insist on policies that support family and work balance.

The Ground Rules: Confronting the Three Dragons— Myths, Fairy Tales, and Stereotypes

I met a single woman for coffee. She had heard about my book from her married-with-children friends and knew I was interested in hearing from women without children, too. Bari had a great career in sales, many friends, and a warm, infectious personality. As she walked into the coffee house, I saw the gaze of several men follow her to our table. This woman had no problem getting dates. I asked Bari what she was looking for in a partner, since she'd expressed slight anxiousness on the phone that at 36, she had no real suitors and hadn't had a serious boyfriend for many years. "I guess that when I was younger, I was looking for someone to take care of me. I had friends who got married to guys that had absolutely no money, and I thought, 'I'd never do that!' I wanted security and someone who was established. But now I see that these couples have built security together—just like I've built my career and made money and bought my own home. I don't need someone to take care of me, but back then it was an idea I had in my head—that I wanted the nice car, the nice house, the option to stay home. . . . And this pretty much eliminated most of the guys my age as potential husbands!"

I asked Bari how her feelings had changed. "Well, I still want men to call me; I never call them. And I want them to pick up the check. But I think I'm more open to meeting men who aren't wealthy, because I have my own security now." Bari, living in a progressive West Coast city, had limited her pool of men practically down to zero—"I think I've met every eligible man in this city!" she joked at one point—because she wanted the Princess Package.

Likewise, a husband I ran into in passing while interviewing his wife, said, "Oh no! Don't let my wife get a copy of that book!" An executive, his career had taken center stage in their relationship for years: His wife played the elegant gourmet hostess to clients and colleagues, she raised their children, and he was free to work long hours and come home to a beautiful home and family when he pleased. But during the interview, his wife expressed cutting resentment. She loved their family life and staying at home but felt her husband minimized her and put himself and his job first, before anything. He was being handed his family life on a silver platter—getting the King of the House treatment—yet I could see that his world was about to be challenged. A strong, no-nonsense woman, his wife was openly discussing her discontent: "He needs to value my contribution and my need for my own life."

Natalie Angier writes, "In examining male and female relationships in various species, only among humans have males succeeded in
stepping between a woman and a meal, in wresting control of the resources that she needs to feed herself and her children. Only among
humans is the idea ever floated that a male *should* support a female,
and that the female is in fact incapable of supporting herself and her
offspring, and that it is a perfectly reasonable act of quid pro quo to
expect a man to feed his family and a woman to be unerringly faithful,
to give the man paternity assurance and make his investment worth-
while."

Even if we are consciously aware of the fairy tales we've grown up
with, the gender-assigned roles for a wife and husband have been
deeply ingrained in our psyches. Harriet Lerner, in *Mother Dance*, describes herself and her husband: "Neither Steve nor I intellectually
embraced the predominant myths of the day: that a mother is her
child's environment, that motherhood is a career rather than a relationship and responsibility, that it's the man's work that really counts,
that a father is and should be the breadwinner, that mothers should
make the sacrifices that children require, that having both children and
career is a given in a man's life and an unrealistic manifestation of
'wanting it all' in a woman's. We were too smart to believe any of
these things, but not smart enough to see how they affected us nev-
ertheless."

So if the inner Princess starts whining for attention, let your husband carry the luggage or give you a backrub—but don't expect that
he take care of you forever after. Living in a tower waiting for rescue
can be quite lonely. You are partners, surely, and each of you will have
times when you're taken care of by the other—that is the gift of mar-

Rate Your Princess or King Behaviors

Who doesn't have a little Princess in them? But is your inner Princess an outer nightmare? Does the King of the House drive everyone out of the house?

- Make a list of your Princess or King of the House behaviors. Focus on your own behavior, looking at both the big picture—for women: I want to be financially taken care of; and the small picture: I never, ever want to touch the garbage. For men, the big picture involves being supported in careers so that they can be unencumbered workers, and the small picture involves expecting others to serve you when you are at home.
- Talk about what's comfortable and uncomfortable for you both. How do you experience the other's behavior? Does it cause pressure, resentment, entertainment value?
- Create a list of what you enjoy doing for each other that might seem "traditional" but is okay with each partner and is a truly giving gesture.

riage. But give up the fairy tales. And for you King of the House types, well, your mother doesn't live here anymore.

INTENTIONAL STEPS TOWARD BALANCING WORK, HOME LIFE, AND MONEY

Our working lives are the area in which many are most willing—and others, most unwilling—to compromise. Following the steps below will help you understand the complexities of your decisions and facilitate mapping new possibilities.

Step One: Value Each Other's Work Goals and Dreams as Equally Important

The summer after my second child was born, I signed up for a class one evening a week. It was important for me to continue my career development and to get out of the house and speak with adults pursuing similar paths. Before I signed up, Gill and I discussed it, since he was working long hours, and it was difficult for him to get home on time. Did it make sense for our schedules? Could the kids live without me for one night? Yes, it could work. We agreed that it was important. For my first class, Gill was late showing up to take the kids. I was late to class. The second class he completely forgot, as I stood in my kitchen, dressed and ready to go, sobbing into the telephone. Furious was an understatement. Not prone to yelling, I yelled. And he let me yell, because he knew he had screwed up. I had reminded him no less than 88 times, but he was so used to coming home from work when he needed to that he couldn't easily adjust to my needs.

This jolted me—and us—into the stark truth: I had no personal freedom, and Gill had lots, even though it included working in a job that he didn't like. In our working lives, it put me into the position of having to request and plead for work time—whether it was going to an early morning meeting or taking a class. There was an imbalance that needed recalibrating. Even though we believed we valued each other's goals, this wasn't being put into active practice. So how do you support your partner?

Ask, listen, and understand. Margaret had two children. She and her husband were financially secure, and she had chosen to stay home with her children for 10 years. She had a timid voice and slightly sloped shoulders; her body language revealed her lack of confidence. "I was an English major and wanted to write, but I did temp work in corporate offices before I had kids. When we got married, it was just assumed that I would stay home and take care of the children. I think that was what appealed to my husband in a way—that I was okay with a stay-at-home wife role to support his career. I expressed vague goals I had for myself. Compared to my husband, who is single-minded and driven, it seemed less important. And Michael rarely asked about what I hoped for my career."

Margaret felt trapped in her current predicament: She was unchallenged and stagnant in her life and yearned for external stimulation—and she felt insecure and vulnerable in a workplace environment. She also believed that her marriage had been stagnant for years, and as a result, her husband had turned a corner and was encouraging her to come up with goals for herself. She was overcoming her reluctance and fears about reentering the working world: "I have just passed a test so I can substitute teach. I applied for an internship at our local newspaper, where I'm competing with high school students for the position! But we're finally having discussions about long-term goals for *me*: What do I want to do 5, 10, and 20 years from now? Now we realize how valuable it is to our kids and our marriage that we both have plans for our own life."

Just articulating dreams can put the process in motion. It weeds out the negative voices—"I can't; I shouldn't; I'm not talented enough; I don't have enough time"—and the guilt. As Maureen Corrigan pointed out in a *New York Times* book review, "The Second Women's Movement may have airlifted a generation of women off their domestic pedestals and dropped them en masse into the workplace, but it doesn't seem to have succeeded yet in persuading a lot of those women and their daughters to stop apologizing for having professional ambition and minds of their own." Our working and exterior lives are a critical part of what makes us whole people. Speak your intention. When I was growing up, my father always said to me "If you have ten dreams and achieve two of them, you're ahead of the game." Share your dreams with your partner, and ask them about theirs.

Take an interest in your partner's goals. "I love it when my husband wants to know all the details of a meeting I had," Leslie, a designer and mother of two, explained. "He'll call me on the phone: 'How did the meeting go? Did they respond well? What did they say?' and he genuinely cares and is interested." When our partners take an active interest in our lives and goals, it fuels our passion. Seeing our partners engaged in achieving goals can renew our relationship and reinvigorate family life. We can help our partners work through blocks, challenge them to meet their goals, and support them when they're down. If you value each other's work and dreams equally, you can provide true support and fulfill your role as true partners. Ask questions, be curious, make suggestions, ask if they want advice, but don't tell them what to do.

Actively support your partner in achieving his goals. Telling our partners we support them is one thing, but actively doing so is another. Active support changes from day to day. It may involve more parenting, less relationship time, driving, covering housework, late night studying sessions, or financial cutbacks and sacrifices. Active support means *doing* beyond just talking.

Lydia, who is an executive and the main breadwinner in her family, says that she would do whatever it takes to support her husband's job as a researcher. "My husband's career is driven by his love of science, which I completely admire. My job is in no way secondary, because I love the field and would do it regardless of the money—but

The Meaning of Work

My Grandpa Sam was orphaned at age 12 with a sixth-grade education. He lived on the streets with his brother, taking any odd job to survive, from shining shoes and cleaning bathrooms to working for a furnace repairman where he had to dive under water in flooded basements to clear drains in order to repair furnaces. His last job was also his best-ever job: he was caretaker of a historical building on the California coast. As soon as we arrived for a visit, we would walk the grounds, often helping him take down the flags at the end of the day. Then he would show us the public restrooms, "You won't find a cleaner bathroom than this." Although he always wished he had a college education, he was proud of his work and saw it as a reflection of himself, his work ethic, and his integrity.

Throughout my life, I've had jobs that were tedious and difficult (although none that come close to Grandpa Sam's experiences)—but I always think of my Grandpa Sam. "Even during the Depression," he would recall, "I could always get a job. I was willing to do the dirty work and do a good job." He taught me that a job well done—no matter the job—deserved respect. He found meaning in his work, however meaningless.

- What meaning can you find in your work—looking at the elements of your emotional, spiritual, physical, and intellectual self?
- What fulfills you about your work? What motivates you?
- Are there people in your life whose work ethic or history influenced you?
- How would you like to fulfill your work potential?

I could easily walk away and find other opportunities. I am supportive of his career endeavors—wherever they may take us—because he has found his calling. If it means moving or changing our lifestyle, I am happy to do it. The passion and energy he brings to his work permeates our family life—and it's wonderful to be able to support that."

Step Two: Understand the Cost of Parenthood

Economics matter on both the small and grand scales; money is so powerful that it truly rules the world. As the wealthiest nation, the United States has become the sole superpower, and many would argue that we have a responsibility to participate in the care and humanitarian concerns of lesser nations, that our abundance should be shared with those less fortunate.

The economics of the household should be held to the same standards. Men have traditionally been in a position of privilege in society. Let's face it: They are in charge of most governments and corporations—both bodies that set policies that alter our family life. Government and the business world passively perpetuate the financial position of men's power by not formally assigning value to the role of stay-at-home parent, by not valuing stay-at-home parents in the gross domestic product, and by failing to provide a support structure for them. Social supports, such as unemployment insurance laws and social security, were enacted in the 1930s for families dependent on a sole breadwinner and remain largely unchanged. They fail to reflect today's current family structure. It's also important to remember that it wasn't until 1993, a mere 10 years ago, that women finally gained a legal right to take a 12-week maternity leave without fear of losing their jobs—although for most, such leaves are still unpaid, and they are not available to some women who work in smaller businesses.

Marriage may be a blessed union of two soul mates, but it isn't necessarily the best financial partnership in town. The cost to women, and men, of being in an unpaid labor force—called parenthood—is tremendous. Often, couples find themselves in an imbalanced situation when one has chosen to stay home or work part-time and one has devoted themselves to a full-time career. This imbalance is manifested over the long term in earning power, retirement income, and self-worth. Many stay-at-home parents who divorce find themselves in financial jeopardy: a mother whose ex-husband refuses to pay child support for his four children or the mother and child who have to move into a one-bedroom apartment after living in a middle-class neighborhood home.

There are real ways to financially protect a parent who is leaving the workforce for a time. Payments can be made into a SEP/IRA for the at-home parent; this parent can be supported in updating their job skills through training, classes, or other means; financial assets can be discussed, understood, and shared by both parents. In this scenario, you are true partners in all ways. In the short term, families can take care of the caretaker by providing financial safeguards, but there is also much we can do to affect the "big picture." If fathers embrace parenting and realize the great social advantage of increased involvement in their children's lives, they can collude with mothers to help change the system. You can do this by:

* Questioning parenting options and nontraditional roles
* Asking employers for family-friendly work policies—and negotiating new and better policies for both your family and others in your workplace

A Husband's Viewpoint

The Gift of Children

To be an equal parent, you have to know what love is, understand how much kids need their father, and know that helping your children grow is the best thing you can do with your time. When I see a father fully present with his child, loving his child, I have these thoughts: Bold. Selfless. Fortunate. Fearless. Look how he openly engages that child, and the child reciprocates tenfold. Successful. He's so successful he's chosen to parent his kids. He's his own man. He ignored the intoxication of some other promise. He knows the gift of children.

❋ Encouraging local and national government to support policies that promote healthy parenting and families

Just as important as men recognizing the opportunities for change is that women create financial independence so they can achieve equality in their homes and the world. When you are financially dependent, or your role providing unpaid labor as a stay-at-home parent isn't valued—by real dollars, not just pats on the back—by your partner or society, then you're in a position of weakness. Financial dependency can be detrimental to mothers, both practically and emotionally. There's no easy solution, and I certainly cannot offer one, except to put forth the challenge to mothers and fathers to join forces and insist that employers and policymakers update policies to support stay-at-home parents, including fathers, in the following areas.

❋ Social security credits for stay-at-home parents
❋ People taxed individually

✳ Subsidized child care

✳ Paid leave for parents of newborns

For further information on areas to press for policy change, look at www.mothersoughttohaveequalrights.org.

How Do You Feel about Money?

Money and sex are notoriously the most common areas of discord in marriage. Money matters—to you, your family, and the world—in all sorts of ways, good and bad. Financial guru Suze Orman recommends, in her useful book *The 9 Steps to Financial Freedom*, that you think back to when you first became aware of money, "... when you began to see that money could create pleasure—ice-cream cones, merry-go-round rides—and also to see that it could create pain—fights between your parents, perhaps, or longings of your own that couldn't be fulfilled, because there wasn't enough money or even because there was too much." Talk with each other about money.

- How did your parents talk about money in front of you? Were you aware of your family's financial situation?
- Did you receive an allowance or earn money as a child?
- Does thinking about money make you feel disgust, worry, greed, fear, guilt, undeservedness?
- Do you constantly feel worried about money? Who did you learn this from?
- Do you feel casual or careless with money? Who did you learn this from?
- What is your spending philosophy? Are you in alignment with your partner's habits?
- How do you feel about your family's current financial situation?

Step Three: Share Financial Knowledge, Decision-Making, and Financial Responsibility

I was speaking with Kathleen, a stay-at-home mother of two, on the phone. Her husband had lost his job in the past week, and I was asking her what their plans were—if they were financially in trouble. "I have no idea," she replied, "Craig handles all of the bill-paying and financial stuff. I couldn't even tell you how much money we have in our bank accounts," she laughed. In a later phone call with her husband, I discovered that he had refinanced their home twice in the past 5 years, pulling money out to cover unsuccessful investments. As a result, Craig said they had no equity in their home, even though they'd owned it for 8 years—and he admitted he was having sleepless nights due to money stress. "I'm a risk-taker in business," he explained, "but probably haven't been responsible enough now that I have a family. Kathleen lets me do whatever I want; She doesn't know what's happening, basically. She has no idea of the state we're in—and it's both our faults. She didn't want to know, and I didn't want her to, either, because then she might have stopped me from risking our money. Of course, now that looks like it might have been the smart thing to do. Be more conservative."

Craig and Kathleen are an extreme example, a carryover from another era when "men handled the finances, and women took care of the home." Kathleen's ignorance about her family's financial position doesn't serve her family, marriage, or herself well. She is shifting all of the emotional burden and responsibility onto her husband—and also allowing him to make decisions *carte blanche*. Meanwhile, Craig has intentionally kept her in the dark; he knew that if she understood what risks he was taking, she would have put her foot down. Kathleen also would have been more than willing to go back to work; she had loved her job as a retail-store manager and had an open invitation to return to work either part- or full-time. Their current predicament may have been avoided if they had practiced these basic fundamentals for a financial partnership.

1. Financial knowledge is shared. It's your job to understand the family finances. Even if you're not the one balancing the checkbook or filling out the loan application, you should be aware of your family's financial situation and the consequences of financial decisions.
2. Financial decisions are made together. From job changes and preschool tuition to refinancing, debt management, and purchases, you share equal decision-making responsibility, no matter who makes the money.
3. Financial responsibility is shared. As equal partners, you must decide together how you will earn money to sustain your lifestyle and raise your children.

As a couple sharing financial responsibility, you provide checks and balances for each other around decision-making. Sometimes it can be frustrating, but there is no place for resentment if you make decisions together. Gill recently wanted to refinance to take advantage of all-time low interest rates, but I was reluctant because we had done so 2 years previously. It took him a month to convince me that it was a sound financial move—and in the meantime, the rate slightly increased. He had spent time showing me the costs of the points and how it would affect our monthly premium. I'm naturally more conservative than he is, and he's more of a risk-taker. Together we create a pretty good team, often saving each other from jumping into decisions because we take the time to discuss and evaluate.

Our Financial Commandments

Pin down your money philosophy, if you haven't already. First, decide how you will share information. When is a good time to pay bills and discuss finances? Gill and I have a standing Tuesday night desk date. We sit at our desk, put on music, and do our best not to treat it as the unwanted stepchild of chores.

Come up with your financial commandments that involve spending, earning, and more. As with all popular commandments, we do our best to follow them. Here are some examples:

1. We agree that with any purchase over X amount, we will consult with our partner.
2. We agree that we will discuss our family finances, including credit card payments, home financing, and budget issues, monthly, quarterly, or other.
3. We agree to discuss major expenditures for the children, such as tuition, child care, school, toys, lessons, and more.
4. We agree that no singular person is accountable for the entire financial burden for the family—decision-making, earning, managing, etc.
5. We agree to file tax returns on time.
6. We agree to be properly insured, including life, auto, health, and property.
7 We agree to keep our priorities clearly in focus.

Final Step: Establish Work and Financial Goals—Together

When you state your intentions by writing down goals, your life-as-it-could-be comes into focus—helping you to exercise the idea of choice, and slowly shaping it into real life. If you keep your goals in mind, your decision-making comes from a different place, influenced by long-term payoffs of fulfillment, time with children, and a lifestyle of your own conscious choosing. If your dreams and goals are valued, it becomes easier to attend to the practical. You may dream about, discuss, and plan improvements on your home: It needs painting; the wood floors need to be refinished; the dishwasher is about to conk out; and there's a leak under the kitchen sink. Of course, the instant gratification of choosing the aesthetic over the structural is hard to resist—the vibrant, new paint or shiny wood floors—but what's wise is maintaining the structure and integrity of your home. Paint looks great, but it cannot hide a leaky roof or plumbing problem.

So, too, we must nurture and preserve the integrity of the family structure. The goals section below is as important as the negotiation points. Our financial and career goals cannot be easily tallied off but must be worked toward systematically, sometimes over a lifetime. Going back to school. Taking a professional exam. Changing careers. Getting out of debt. All take time and commitment. Begin by clarifying specific goals and renewing purpose in relation to your working lives. Use the points below to help you get started.

Work goals related to parenting: This may mean flex-time, a move to part-time, or work at home 1 day a week.

Career goals: These may include a pay raise, new job, career change, going to a 3-day workweek, or taking a 2-year sabbatical.

Career development: What are you doing to stimulate yourself and your career? This can include learning a new trade, classes, and informational interviews, or volunteering in a setting where you learn something new. Maybe there is an area in your job that seems insurmountable—such as sales presentations—and taking a public speaking course or signing up for Toastmasters is the ticket.

Education: This could call for going back to school, evening classes, trade school, or an apprenticeship or internship.

Use the chart below as an example of how you and your partner can outline your specific goals.

Who	Goal	Timeframe
Sue	Take Toastmasters to work on public speaking	Sept–Nov
Sue	Work toward more responsibility in job; ask for 10 percent pay raise	April
Sue	Work from home 1 day per week	now
Kevin	Go down to 30-hour workweek	Sept
Kevin	Find more consulting clients	Nov–Dec

Part of our responsibility as adults is creating financial security for our families and futures—to the best of our ability. This doesn't mean living in fear around finances or feeling that at any moment you could be on the streets if you don't have a huge nest egg that will catch you if you fall. What financial responsibility means is taking stock of your finances and your earning power and putting money in the right buckets. It means making sure that if something happens to you or your partner, the financial means are available to help see your children through to adulthood. It is your responsibility to save for your child's education—and it's your responsibility to take care of yourself by putting away money for your retirement. What if, instead of choosing to spend money on dozens of Barbies and things for our children, we instead put money every month into a tax-free educational fund? Ask each other what your ideal financial goals are. Let the following areas help get your conversation started.

Monthly budgeting: paying bills, preparing for taxes, managing spending

Retirement/investing: managing 401(k), IRA, or other retirement fund contributions, mutual funds, stocks and brokerage accounts, meeting with financial consultant

Education funds: researching funds, understanding tax ramifications, managing contributions, monthly automatic deposits

Managing debt: loan applications, refinancing, home equity loans, credit card balances

Insurance: life insurance, auto and property insurance, specific regionally needed insurance, such as flood and earthquake

Wills: estate planning, designating power of attorney, who will take care of your children, setting up trusts, etc.

The chart below gives some examples of how you might outline the financial goals you've set as a couple.

Who	Goal	Timeframe
Sue/Kevin	Pay off credit cards	June–Aug
Kevin	Reallot retirement accounts to medium risk portfolio	NOW
Sue	Finish will!	NOW

NEGOTIATION POINTS

When you look at the financial items below, remember that although one of you may "own" the task, you must still share financial knowledge and decision-making. With your financial responsibilities and assigning ownership, also keep in mind the why: Are you in charge of this item because of time, expertise, or a desire to learn? Make sure that your intentions are not coming from a desire to control or yield power over the other, keep secrets, or micromanage.

Financial Task	Owner	Frequency
Monthly budgeting		
Pay monthly bills		
Organize family files		
Health insurance management		
Education savings plans		
Retirement savings plans		
Insurance management		
Insurance claims		
Tax preparation		
Will preparation		
Financial relationships		
Meet with broker		
Meet with financial planner		
Meet with tax accountant		
Meet with insurance agent		
Banking contact		

INTENTION: COMMIT TO SUPPORTING EACH OTHER'S WORKING AND EXTERIOR LIFE

In the end, one of the cornerstones of equal parenting is equally valuing the goals of each individual, whether it's the dream of being a stay-at-home parent or the dream of being a designer or manager.

For those couples that choose to have a primary parent who stays home, it's critical that the child care role carries equal weight, financially and otherwise, in the relationship. And it's important to make sure the stay-at-home parent doesn't permanently release their dreams and goals.

Managing Work and Money Intention Statement:

We commit to equally valuing each other's working life and sharing responsibility for decision-making related to work and family finances.

_____   _____
Signed   Signed

CHAPTER 5

Raising the Children

If you want your children to succeed,
show them how to fail.
If you want them to be happy,
show them how to be sad.
If you want them to be healthy,
show them how to be sick.
If you want them to have much,
show them how to enjoy little.

—William Martin, *The Parent's Tao Te Ching*

The path of parenting has lots to do with how you handle the inevitable—the work and emotions of raising children. We may fight it, embrace it, hide from it, but the reality of parenting is that you are, first and foremost, grown-ups making grown-up decisions. There are moments, too many to count, when we have a parenting epiphany, a flash of insight about why life works the way it does. The epiphanies are often humdrum—the sudden understanding of why so many people have minivans, shop at Costco, and go to bed at 9:30 P.M. But the epiphanies are also powerful, such as understanding the depth of love parents hold for children or knowing that—as everyone insisted on telling you before your child came into your life—life as you once knew it has changed forever.

Your relationship and how you parent together form the heart of your household. Are you in couple harmony? Do you cherish and appreciate each other's contribution? Are your parenting styles and expectations in sync? Parenting can mean two different things to each partner. For one, spending the night parenting while another is working late might involve preparing a healthy dinner, picking up the house, getting ready for school the next day, and putting the kids to bed shiny-clean and on time. For the other partner, parenting may simply mean showing up: A frozen dinner, no bath, a quick tooth brushing, and falling asleep on the couch in front of the television may seem like perfectly acceptable parenting.

Parenting is more than showing up, though. Diapering a child isn't just a simple little wipe to those cute cheeks and a quick change. It's knowing when the diapers, the wipes, and the diaper rash cream are about to run out and buying more. It's taking out the trashcan when the aroma starts to call out to the small, wild animals in the neighborhood—or taking the graduate course in Diaper Genie management. It's getting Balmex, because you know that's the one that works best on your kid. It's putting diapers in the diaper bag when you leave the house—and stashing an emergency diaper kit in the car, the swim bag, and the stroller. It's knowing diaper sizes and brands, how to pull and place the tabs so there's no leakage, or how to finesse cloth diapers with Velcro covers that make your kid's booty look humungous. It's knowing the "signs" of movement. And it's putting on new clothes after a big blowout. Changing the diapers includes knowing the tricks to entertain your child, the toys to place in their hands and the particular wrestling hold that keeps them from rolling over or away. It's the time spent away from the adults in the other room, giving big belly kisses to keep your baby, and yourself, laughing. It's not only about changing the diapers but about changing your attitude, your pace, and your relationship with all things poop-related. Before you can become truly equal parents, you must ask not just who changes the diapers in your family (or who packs the lunch or drives carpool) but who does all the behind-the-scenes chores that make it possible to change the diapers.

Parenting roles are slowly expanding beyond the "I've changed my share of diapers" line. Larry, who works full-time, reports on his nighttime duty with his two children. "I wake up instantly, and Jackie just keeps snoring," he says, amused. More and more fathers pick their children up from school or drive carpool, although they're still firmly in the minority. Last week I overheard my husband reciting the weight variance for diaper sizes to one of his friends, as they were admiring the friend's newborn baby. I suspect he was flaunting his parenting know-how. We are on the brink of change, as fathers are more involved than ever, paying attention to the details, taking on more responsibility, and forming close ties with their children. Yet men are still not as inclined as women to alter their careers and schedules to formally participate in the lives of their children.

During an interview with a small group of women, I asked them to discuss their current child care situation and how it came to be. Peggy, a stay-at-home mother of three boys under age six, laughed and said, "What child care help? Me and them. Twenty-four hours a day. It's what's best for my children—I *want* to be home." A full-time working mother, Joelle, responded, "Well, I work and travel a lot. I have a full-time nanny about 50 to 60 hours a week, who my son

Raising the Children Quiz

Like friendly but insistent aliens, your children take over your body and then your life. The hard part about parenting isn't the loving them when they're cute 2-year-olds part, or coaching a sport, or watching a school play. Those are the rewards of parenting. The difficult part is the constant organizing, the relentless work, and of course the emotional strain that comes with trying to understand how to parent children in the best way possible, so that our children may thrive. Take this quiz as a couple.

1. How many times have you cut out of work because of pinkeye, a parent-teacher conference, or a school field trip?

2. Recite the phone numbers for the pediatrician, your top two babysitters, your children's best friends, and the therapist.

3. How much lead time do you need for a kid haircut appointment at the local barbershop? A birthday party invite? To cancel a piano lesson without penalty?

4. What are the current modes of discipline employed in your family? Rank in order of effectiveness. (If none are effective, join the club!)

5. What are the emotional states of your children today? What's the next emotional hurdle or anxiety-producing challenge ahead?

loves and who is absolutely wonderful." Joelle squirmed, as if embarrassed, as she described a job that she was passionate about and paid very well. I asked her if she felt judged by other mothers. "Oh, all the time—at least in my community, which has lots of stay-at-home moms—but sometimes I wonder if it's imagined, their criticisms, or if it's just my guilt making me paranoid. I do get mixed reactions from men, either 'What kind of woman would leave her child and go on a 10-day business trip?' or admiration that I'm successful and ambitious.

6. Beyond videos, name one activity that would engross your child for 30 minutes.

7. If your child is a teenager, name the outfit that drives you crazy, what most induces the eye roll, and their most visited Web site. Now speculate on what they do behind their closed bedroom door. Scary, huh?

8. List the top three foods your child will eat that have nutritional value.

9. List the steps of making your child's lunch in under 3 minutes, with no peanut butter or bread in the house (not that peanuts are allowed in schools).

10. Who most recently sorted through old clothes? Old toys?

11. Who has most recently lain in bed holding your child when she couldn't get to sleep or woke up with a nightmare?

12. Count up your volunteer hours this month at school, overseeing homework, and coaching.

13. Think of five questions to ask when interviewing a babysitter, nanny, or school teacher.

14. Think of one real question to ask your child that they might answer with enthusiasm.

Luckily, my husband has a flexible job with no travel—so he can leave work at 5:00 and cover for me."

I pointed out to all the women in the group that, except for Joelle, no one had discussed their husband's role in the day-to-day demands of raising the children. "Where's dad?" I ventured. Peggy responded, "My husband works long hours. On the weekends he's a pretty involved dad, although he definitely requires downtime from his job." She explained that her husband often went out alone a couple of times on the weekends—for coffee or to meet a friend or grab a beer in the evening—to get alone time. The other mothers sighed and expressed their own need and longing for that "alone time." Another mother pointed out that Peggy's husband was "awfully lucky" to be able to go out whenever he felt like it—and Peggy defended her situation: "He gets very difficult if he doesn't have his own time." "Maybe you should get very difficult yourself," the group challenged. During the heated dialogue, Joelle was silent. When asked her opinion, she sheepishly admitted, "I guess I'm the one in our relationship that gets the alone time." Joelle's business travel allowed her personal freedom in the evenings to work out, go to restaurants, watch movies in her hotel room, even shop leisurely for clothes on occasion. "I'm working, of course, but it's like a vacation sometimes, if you want to know the truth."

From Peggy, who was considering home schooling her three boys, to Joelle, who was about to begin a 2-month "career-maker" overseas assignment, the variations in mothers' lives are vast. Although they characterized them as loving, emotionally engaged fathers, the majority of the women in my interview groups described their husbands as lacking a formal role in raising their children. Whether working outside the home or not, mothers are generally the primary parents, making decisions about day care, preschool and playdates; carpooling; helping with homework; taking kids to the doctor; sorting through clothes and toys; and dealing with the minutiae of child-raising. And while our husbands may be more emotionally present and involved than the previous generation of fathers, roughhousing and tickling children are only a small fraction of what it means to be a parent. It is mothers and other care providers who do most of the planning and organizing of their child's lives.

Quick Tips

If child care issues, whether for babies or teens, have led you to an impasse with your mate, or you're overcome with frustration or hopelessness, here are four things in this chapter that might have the most immediate impact.

1. Do the "Imagine the Possibilities" exercise on page 160.
2. Define what good parenting means to you.
3. Read the section titled "Let Go of Being the Boss Parent" on page 168.
4. Go to the "Creating Intention Statements" section on page 182 with your partner.

For some, this is a conscious choice and decision, and they feel supported in this role; others complain bitterly about the double duty of work and parenting, but cannot let go. "Despite our rhetoric to the contrary, most women continue to undermine and undercut the attempts of their men to even up the domestic score," Susan Maushart explains in *The Mask of Motherhood*, "This is particularly the case when it comes to the day-to-day management of our children's lives. As inexplicable or even as embarrassing as it may be, the fact is that most mothers—regardless of our professional status—still insist on nonnegotiable oversight of our kids' meals, clothing, homework, television viewing, bedtimes, and a host of other mundane but somehow sacred spheres of domestic influence."

As you read this chapter, stand back and look at the parenting landscape you currently inhabit—and define the one you'd like to live in together in the future.

HOW DO WE WANT TO RAISE
OUR CHILDREN?

Public opinion still believes that it's better if a parent, especially the mother, is able to stay home for at least the first years of a child's life. Opinion is a distant country from Reality though, as the majority of children under age six are in some form of child care—and mothers overwhelmingly want to continue working. Many studies have come out in the past 10 years with alarmist headlines—*Working Mothers Ruining Children* or *Children in Daycare More Violent!*—constantly making women question their choices. But studies that examine the consequences of the working father on a child rarely surface, and when they do, they lack the same political weight or opportunity for misuse.

Despite what public opinion and sensational headlines imply, the problem isn't with working parents as much as it is a problem with working parents' options. The age-old expression, "It Takes a Village to Raise a Child," assumes that a child is surrounded—and a mother is supported—by a community. A tribe, a parenting group, relatives, nannies, day care centers—whatever you call the village, children have been raised by a collective effort of care providers from time immemorial. In a report on "Childcare and Our Youngest Children," authors Deborah Philips and Gina Adams concluded that "there is a mismatch between the rhetoric of parental choice and the realities facing parents of young children in the United States."

Most parents don't have natural support networks, such as a tribe or extended family, ready to pick up the toddlers and guide the children—so we must rely on outside paid help. Many parents, usually those making higher incomes, have access to better day care. But few families have the money to hunt for the best nanny in town. As Stanley Greenspan, M.D. points out, "We often try to reassure ourselves that there are day care providers and centers that do provide good nurturing, but the vast majority of institutional and family day care is not of high quality . . . It's important to point out . . . that the dilemma in child care is not the parents' fault, and in many respects it's not the fault of child care providers either . . . we may simply be asking the day care system to do too much: We are expecting it to operate the way very well-functioning families do."

Where does this leave us? We want our children as well-cared-for as possible. Loved. Stimulated. Safe. Healthy. Warm and fed. But everyone has different requirements—from financial to emotional— that dictate our child care situations. Respecting our unique choices

A Frank Discussion on Child Care

Depending on the age of your children, decisions lie ahead about how to care for them. Have a heart-to-heart with your partner about how you feel about the following:

- Day care in general
- The best child care environment for small children
- Involvement in your child's daily life once they begin school
- After-school care
- Babysitters or in-home nannies
- Family members sharing in the care of your children
- Trading the primary parenting role throughout your child's life
- What fears do you have about day care? What fears do you have about no child care help?
- What fears do you have about not being home after school?
- What do you love about what's working now, and what could improve?

Imagine the Possibilities

Write about your perfect parenting scenario, including time spent with children, your partner's involvement, and both of your working lives. How does your life unfold as your children grow?

is just as important as joining together to work toward a common goal of valuing the "job" of child care, whether provided by parents, family, or a child care provider. Changing public policy and corporate-culture ideals about child care is paramount—and right now, we can focus on how we want to parent our kids and how two parents can find the best solution possible.

THE EQUAL PARENTING AGREEMENT FOR RAISING THE CHILDREN

We commit to intentionally designing our parenting roles and being equally responsible for child care and child-related tasks.

How you take care of your children—and how you can do so as a collaborative couple—sets the tone for their lives. From a balanced marriage to a healthy home and hearth to the community around them, we strive to give our children our best. It is a vow we make to them when they come into this world and are first sheltered in our welcoming arms. Treat this chapter as precious. As you state your parenting intentions, stay the course, and share in the love and work of parenting.

Before You Begin: Redefining the Good Mother and Good Father

Modern motherhood is lived out under microscopic scrutiny, with most mothers willingly pursuing the cultural ideal of "the Good Mother." Rosalind Barnett and Caryl Rivers point out that "blaming mom has become as American as apple pie. Psychologists Paul and Jeremy Caplan say that 'mother blame' is rampant in our culture and in the sciences. When they examined 125 articles written for professional journals, they discovered mothers were blamed for 72 kinds of problems in their offspring, ranging from bedwetting to schizophrenia." It's no wonder women have embraced the Mother Martyr role, believing they're singularly responsible for the health and well-being of their children. It explains why mothers sit in a pool of guilt, feeling responsible for and overanalyzing everything from their child's table manners to tantrums to high school report cards.

It also helps to explain the current wrestling match as women reject the good mother definition of yesteryear—an unattainable role based on sacrificing all for their children—and define today's less precise, more well-rounded definition of a good mother. Alisa, a working mother of two school-age children, explains that she works at home 40 hours a week and manages the bulk of the day-to-day child-related tasks. "I know this sounds quaint, but I want to make cookies for my kids after school and drive them where they need to go and be a part of their lives." She feels the pull of both worlds, "I know it's lucky I work at home—sometimes!!—and I have a good salary to contribute to the family. I love my work and actually cannot wait to get back into a job that's out of the house." She worries that if she isn't working at home, though, she is a bad mother. "I can't help but remember my mom and how she was home after school—and that's the way it should be. Even when she worked part-time, she always had hours that coincided with our school hours."

We have worked hard to construct our lives in ways that are best for us—refashioning our ideas of what good parenting truly means. Bonny, a full-time working mom, shares her definition: "A good mother shares and instills values within her children, can nurture all of their needs accordingly, and can help to raise independently creative, curious, thoughtful, loving, and fun people. She's someone who can be as supportive to their partner and other family members as to their kids—and someone that can truly love herself and emulate what a happy and fulfilled person is to those around them. The same for a good father! I think even though there are distinct roles we each play, it's based on what's right for the kids and household—not based on gender rules."

Deirdre, a stay-at-home mother of two, adds, "Good mothers are warm and responsive but also set limits where appropriate and have reasonable but high expectations for their children's behavior. They have goals for their children—to be independent, caring, happy, achievement-oriented, and so forth—and actively help their children meet those goals. They keep their children's best interests in mind at all times, but do not let the children run their parents' lives. I also think playfulness and flexibility are very important qualities of a good mother. Good mothers have respect for their children's desires and encourage them to express themselves. I think being able to assume your child's perspective and to consider her point of view (but not necessarily acquiescing to every demand) is essential to being a good parent." Jim, a full-time working father of two, says, "A good father is someone who is comfortable with his emotions, someone who can openly display affection toward his children and his partner. He is someone who really takes the time to understand and connect with his child and who continues to foster his relationships on a deep level inside and outside of the home."

What is strikingly modern about these definitions is that not one references breadwinning or homemaking; quality parenting today means nurturing children, instilling values, and modeling healthy behavior. Our definition of the "good parent" has expanded and been made contemporary—mothers are whole people; fathers can be emotionally in touch—but there is a holdover. Women, in particular, still express regret over not fulfilling the traditional definition of the good mother, even if that definition was not based on reality and even if they have little or no interest in staying at home to parent. From baking cookies to PTA participation, working mothers feel mild pangs of guilt that they are not always there for their children. Fathers, on the other hand, feel generally good about their roles: They are much more involved than their own fathers were and certainly help out around the house more. Interestingly, as parenting roles have evolved, mother's roles have become more exterior—about expanding out into the world—while father's roles have become more interior—involved in their home lives and exploring emotional territory.

We have qualities that come naturally to us; arguably they might be gender-based, but more likely they are socialized behaviors—the quirks of our own personality—or learned from our family of origin or cultural icons. As Natalie Angier explains in her remarkable book, *Woman*, "Look at the male rat. A male rat does not normally care for newborn pups. Fatherly devotion is not in the standard contract. Yet he has the raw goods of affection. If you put a young male rat into an enclosure with a litter of newborns and give him a chance to grow accustomed to their smells and hear their squeaks, he will eventually start

Calling Out the "Good Parent"

The mere notion of good mothering and good fathering begs the question: Why should they be any different? Create in your family a good-parenting definition—one to which you will both aspire, knowing each may excel in different areas. Answering the questions below is a start.

- How will you model good behavior?
- How will you help your children feel loved?
- How will you make your children feel safe and secure?
- How will you support your child's individuality?
- How will you nurture learning, creativity, and physical activity?

nuzzling them. He'll huddle over them and lick them. If one should stray from the nest, he'll retrieve it. He has fallen in love with a pile of squirming pink pencil erasers." But Angier warns, "An essential factor in the experiment: The mother rat must be removed from the scene, for if she were there, she would sooner kill the male than allow him near her young." Despite the gains we have made, the evolution of human relationships and parenting doesn't seem so far removed. We must fully accept the notion that good parenting isn't the exclusive territory of either gender.

The Ground Rules: Equal Responsibility for Raising the Children

"As long as I know that one day it's 'my turn' again, then I can take a few years off," said Steve. He and his wife, Estrella, were both CPAs at big firms, until he was laid off. Her solo income could cover the family finances with some modest budgeting, and Steve discovered that, far from being "unemployed," he liked staying home and managing the house and their two kids' lives. "This year, I've been the soccer coach for my daughter and the assistant track coach for my son; I've memorized Marcella Cucina and can cook some mean Italian

Walk a Mile in the Other Parent's Shoes

An exercise for the primary breadwinner: Imagine that you are a stay-at-home parent and have just taken care of a newborn and toddler for 12 hours—the time it takes your spouse to commute and work a 10-hour day. You must properly feed, clothe, and entertain your children throughout the day, paying attention to developmentally appropriate activities, naps, moods, and the like. Also, you must consider grocery shopping, laundry, kitchen cleanup and a household pickup; make dinner; and have a playdate for your toddler. You did manage to take a shower, but your hair is uncombed, and you are wearing a gray sweatshirt and jeans christened with spit-up and yogurt. How do you feel when your spouse walks through the door?

Exercise for the primary parent: Imagine that you have just worked a 12-hour day; stood on commute trains or driven in bumper to bumper traffic; sat in a 3-hour-long meeting that drained the lifeblood out of you; suffered through a boss's panicky, cruel outburst; completed three project deadlines at the very last minute with people breathing down your neck; and tried for an hour to leave the office so that you could see your spouse and children, while people kept interrupting you with "emergencies." How do you feel as you walk through the door, your partner hands you a crying baby, and your toddler is instantly hanging on your leg?

If neither of these scenarios seem appealing to you—the utterly exhausted parent versus the uptight, stressed-out worker—discuss what does sound appealing.

Discuss What Equal Responsibility Means to You

Parenting your children involves all sorts of things—going without sleep, fore-going job promotions, overtime pay, a workout at the gym, material things....
True partnership lies in being equally responsible for raising your children. Write down the methods and practices you think can keep you committed to the idea of intentional parenting.

meals. And I think I'm a much better housekeeper than my wife, frankly. Once I got over the shame I felt about getting laid off after a 20-plus-year career, I realized I had an opportunity to get to know my kids really well. They will be off to college soon, and I will have had this special time with them. I can always work, and I don't miss the stress from working. Sometimes it's hard with particular fathers, they look at you like you're kind of pathetic, but most fathers are envious that I'm relaxed and so close to my kids. Our family is close; my marriage is stronger than ever. There's the payoff."

Steve and Estrella, by default they admit, treated their parenting responsibilities equally: They were both breadwinners and parents in their minds. When Steve lost his job, he naturally took over most of the household duties and discovered that he liked it—and that he liked participating in his kids' lives and volunteering in the community. They had the luxury of having one parent stay home, if they so chose, but they also had an outlook that assumed they were both making equal sacrifices. Steve admits, "If I hadn't seen Estrella take off a few years when our kids were born and reenter the workforce going gang-busters, maybe I'd be more nervous."

INTENTIONAL STEPS TOWARD
RAISING THE CHILDREN

Following the steps below will help you negotiate the crazy, rocky, and delightful road of parenting with your partner.

Step One: Share the Responsibility for Child Care Equally

It's time to debunk the idea that only "mother knows best." This keeps women locked into the laundry room and men locked out—and by now we know just how much we need their help. Sharing the responsibility of child care means not making assumptions, devaluing our partner's life path, or taking on responsibility for the wrong reasons.

Determine your child care and schooling needs together. After taking your work lives into account, discuss, negotiate, and agree upon how you would like to parent your children, given your financial needs. Dina explains, "Before we had our first child, we discussed thoroughly how we would handle the day-to-day situations. I'm pretty anal (I'm a scientist!) about those kinds of things, and so I really needed to figure it all out. We've made adjustments many times, based on where we were from a job perspective or day care perspective. At the time of our son's birth, my husband was in graduate school, and thus I knew I had to continue back to work to help support us. Knowing this helped to relieve some of the pressure about whether to stay at home or not. It wasn't a choice."

Share responsibility for finding and managing child care and school. From full-time baby care to after-school care to date night, who grabs the phone to call the babysitter? Agree on who will have the primary relationship with each care group—and how the responsibility will be shared. When I was working at home, it made sense for me to drop off and pick up my daughter from school, but I wanted Gill to participate—because it was an important milestone to see our daughter coming and going to and from school and because I needed Gill to contribute so I could get to work early one morning a week. He took over with both children, managed the breakfast and lunch routine, and took Ella to school. When later, the tables turned, and I was the one with the full-time job, Gill negotiated with me to do the same for him, so that he could get in extra morning hours.

Let Go of Being the Boss Parent

Often it's hard for mothers to let go of the 24/7 nature of mothering and entrust their partners with the mental obsession that overtakes many a formerly sane mind. Maybe we're afraid to let go of our primary parent power because we feel we've given up other sources of power—financial independence and control or our freedom—so we believe our only place of power resides in controlling the home front.

Here's a secret: He *can* do it! Everything will not go perfectly all the time. Your spouse will make mistakes, just as we all make mistakes, and then learn from them. Keep your judgments in check and support your partner's parenting.

- Don't undermine the other parent
- Avoid criticizing or hovering
- Let them discover for themselves
- Don't rescue unless necessary
- Appreciate their unique parenting style
- Learn from each other
- Discuss expectations beforehand
- Remember to stay on the same team

Share information—and listen. Having good parenting information drives good parenting. You might be the parent who knows that your daughter gets a stomachache when she eats pancakes or that your son had an incident at school that made him sad and lonely—and sharing this information with your mate allows them to know and care for your children better. No detail is too small: Did they drink enough milk and eat enough green vegetables this week? Did they have a late nap? Maybe your teenager received a low grade on a test, and this is why he's in his room with the door closed and a "do not disturb" sign on it. Remember to talk with each other about your children's world—and to listen.

Step Two: Find Common Ground

Cyril is a stay-at-home father taking care of an 18-month-old daughter, while his wife works full-time. A large man, and gruff at first impression, his demeanor is more "gentle Ben" than grizzly bear once he relaxes. As his daughter bounces off his lap and around the room, he handles her like fine china, clearly in tune with her behavior patterns and needs. He registers his complaint, "Every weekend it's the same thing," he says, "I have a routine in place—naps, eating, bottles, a bedtime ritual—and my wife comes home and wreaks havoc on our system! She gives Stella a bottle whenever she whines for it; she doesn't put her down for a nap the right way. She totally indulges her." Cyril's concerns are common to the primary parent, although I generally hear them expressed by women. "Come Monday," he explains, "I have to start all over, and she's more sensitive and tired when not on her regular schedule."

It is important to be in agreement on some family standards. Each parent has different styles that add character and color to your family, but kids thrive with some routine and consistent messages. It's frustrating to come home from a night out and find the children up late, eating a barrel of chocolate ice cream, with the house a mess. It can cause a rift between parents and is the cause for many a complaint, from "He always feeds the kids junk food," to "They watch too many videos with her." To eliminate misunderstandings and parent more effectively, it helps to discuss and be in cahoots on the areas below.

Nutrition: What will you feed your kids, and how will you teach them about healthy eating? Determine your food philosophy re-

Routines Leave Room for Adventure

My Grandma Janet, a woman almost 6 feet tall at a time when women were not supposed to be tall, was long-legged and full of resourcefulness, a get-up-and-go attitude, and love for the Dodgers. She laughed easily but was stern with her list of do's and don'ts that showed your character: You must like fresh tomatoes from her garden; iron your clothes, brush your hair, and tuck in your shirt; and please, stop your complaining, for it's a waste of time. She once told me when I was complaining about work stress: "It's funny, we never had the word 'stress' in my time." In other words, they just sucked it up and did it.

For my grandparents, the process of life was enjoyable. Preparing meals, gardening, bedtime, the tradition of sitting down before a meal with a drink and cheese and crackers—they relished these moments and went through them with ease, or so it appeared to us grandkids. Adventures did not have to be grand. Special moments could be found anywhere.

One of the most impressionable moments with my Grandmother, one that she

garding sugar, organic products, dessert, junk food, fast food, meal-time, and snack time.

Discipline: What techniques do you use? What are the rules you want to adopt for your household? Agree on boundaries and discipline.

Routine: What structure would you like around bedtime, tooth brushing, television watching, homework, phone calls, computer time, curfews, and driving. Agree on what's most important.

Behavior: What will you teach regarding manners, how you treat people, tone of voice, language, school behavior, and dress?

barely remembers but I'll remember forever, happened when I was 4 years old. Always put to work in the garden weeding, I found it wasteful to just throw all of the weeds away. These were weeds that I had carefully pulled, bringing every stubborn root with them, in order to free up my crowded, succulent garden vegetables. I carefully lined up the weeds, sorry to throw them out—when a thought struck me. Why couldn't we eat these weeds? Why not, really? I told my Grandmother my thought, and she said what a fine idea this was. We must first boil them to make them tender, and then we would feast on them. I carefully cleaned them and decided that it was the roots that looked most edible. So we cut off the greens. We boiled the roots.

Sitting side by side, we each took a forkful of our first taste of cooled down roots served on proper plates. Chewing, my Grandma said, "Salt," and I replied, "Yes, salt." We pretended the salt made the weeds edible. "Well, what do you think?" she asked me when we had finished a plate. "They taste like dirt." And we both began laughing, thrilled with our small adventure, despite its outcome, or maybe because of the outcome.

Step Three: Commit to Your Family; Spend the Time

In a study conducted by Colorado State University, interviewing 47 dual-earner couples about how they successfully managed their lives, one of the findings was about the level of family commitment and how it was put into practice: "These couples emphasized family happiness over professional responsibilities and advancement. In fact, they often discussed employment as a means for ensuring family well-being. It was not uncommon for participants to limit work hours, sacrifice career advancement, make career changes, or accept less-prestigious positions to keep family as the number one priority in life."

Commitment to family can mean real sacrifices. Albert, the father of three children, held a midlevel sales manager position for 8 years, because it didn't involve lots of travel. He explains, "During that period, when my children were born and as they were beginning school, I turned down two promotions and two outside job offers, because they would have equaled lots more time on the road and possibly moving my family. I knew two things: I wanted to be around to see my kids every single day; and I wanted to support my wife as much as possible. Time on the road was very difficult for my wife with three young children. Turning down promotions was hard on me, I won't lie, and the company gave me a tough time, pressuring me from all sides. My wife and I made a decision that time was more important than money, but I still got frustrated that people less experienced than me started becoming my bosses and making more money. That was the choice I made though, and I'm glad I did." Albert goes on to explain that once his kids were older, he did begin to take the promotions and shot quickly up the corporate ladder. "It's like I was being held back," he says, "and then was shot out of a cannon. And now I'm pushing back at work again to make sure I'm putting my kids first. It's tough, but I'm so connected to my kids now that I can't stand to miss out on their lives."

Sunday morning waffle breakfasts or Thanksgiving hikes—rituals and activities punctuate our commitment in a profound, special, and concrete way. Simple rituals can make lasting impressions: My mother always sang, "Oh, what a beautiful morning!" to wake us up before school. Although we would cry out in protest—"Stop, Mom! Just 15 more minutes of sleep!"—I was always smiling into my pillow at my mother's insistence on starting each day this way. A grandfather recently explained his life philosophy to me, "I have three wonderful

Don't Forget to Play

Ella and I were sitting at the dinner table together when she announced that barbequed ribs were her favorite food. "Wow," I said. "When I was a little girl, ribs were my favorite food, too." She looked at me curiously. "Mom, I wish you were a little girl now so we could play together." I was struck by the simple sweetness of her wish—and also by the sadness. Why did I have to be a little girl to play? I use my "mom firm voice" almost all the time and often wind up multitasking, doing chores and errands instead of being present with my children. I get so focused on the doing—brush your teeth, eat your veggies, have good table manners—that I forget to play. Playing with my children is the joyful part of parenting—and the creative, joyful part of myself that I like the most.

How can you remember to play with your kids today?

children and two grandchildren who love their Grandpappy to death. I'm so blessed. Life is good for me and my family—and that's what it's all about, loving your kids and family well."

Step Four: Respect Your Child's Style

Families fall into two categories: the calendar family or the laissez-faire family. We have friends in both camps. If we want to see our friends Edwina and Chris, we have to book about 2 months in advance, and if we're lucky they are free, and we get to enjoy them. Other friends we can call that day, "Hey, want to come over for a casual barbeque?" And they're free, like us. It's just family style and family culture. One makes for a full, interesting, runaround life; and the other is about spontaneity, relaxing, and space.

The same holds true for our children's lives. Some kids are booked solid with lessons, playdates, museum trips, and music lessons, and other children prefer a quieter schedule. Greta, a mother of two children, who balanced a career, children, and active social life, had two children who were polar opposites, as she explains: "I'm a go-go-go type person, and my firstborn, my son, was this way also. He played in the school band and did Boy Scouts and crew and public speaking competitions. I thought this was great and natural, and weren't all kids like this?!" Five years later, she had a daughter, "and my second only wanted to focus on one thing at a time. From about age 7 to 13 it was ballet. I encouraged her to take a sport, music lessons, anything—and she was very comfortable and determined to focus exclusively on ballet. Now, it's boys—one boy in particular—and I'm freaked!" Greta realizes that her style isn't necessarily right for her daughter—yet she also wants to instill a sense of their

A Husband's Viewpoint

The Risk and Reward
of Fatherhood

I'm driving in the car, and my son, Matthew, makes a raspberry sound and I mimic it, and he laughs, and I laugh back at him. And then we're trading laughs as we cruise down the road. I'm amazed at how right this feels to me. I never would have had this moment if I hadn't taken the risk to be here. I get this exchange of pure love, because I chose it. Did I choose it at a cost to myself? To my career? Perhaps, for everything has a cost. Yet I don't feel the need to measure what that cost might be. For I know that this moment is priceless.

family values, beyond boys, in her daughter and expose her to culture, nature, and outdoor activities. As a compromise, Greta and her daughter have agreed to go to the ballet several times a year, that her daughter continue one dance class, and that they will go on a 2-week family camping trip this summer.

It's your job to honor your kids' needs and parent them in the way they need to be parented. While modeling values, you also want to put them into practice, all the while conscious of the fine line between teaching and exposing our children to a variety of experiences and not putting our expectations on them. There's nothing worse for a child than a parent who sets their sights on vicarious achievement through their son or daughter. During my soccer playing days in Junior High, one girl on our team had a father who would run onto the field and argue with the refs, our coach, and even the other players on the field. He was determined that his daughter would be a soccer star and failed to notice that she was humiliated each time he acted out in this way.

Step Five: Improve Parenting Skills and Emotional Intelligence—Together

Even as parents are taken to task about balancing work and family, we must also cautiously tiptoe through the parenting skills minefield. New parents, baby boomer parents, parents of teenagers—all are reading books and magazine articles, talking to the pediatrician, and comparing notes with other parents to try to deliver high-tech, high-touch Extreme Parenting. Just trying to choose topics for nighttime reading—nonviolent communication, building self-esteem, sleeping through the night, 100 ways to love a teenager, or avoiding TV violence—is enough to send you to bed with a migraine. The messages, from useful to white noise to junk, assault us from all directions and drown out our own intuition. Whether you like Sears or Brazelton, practice attachment parenting or are now "babywise," you worry that you haven't read the right book at the right time with the right messages.

Psychologist David Anderegg spells it out in his book, *Worried All the Time*, explaining that parents today worry more than those of yesteryear. "This is the phenomenon I call 'overparenting,'" he says, "overthinking, overworrying, and eventually, overreacting . . . Overparenting is trying to make perfect decisions every single time in a world that is much more indeterminate and forgiving than most parents believe." It takes confidence, years of parenting, and a little attitude to turn your back on the parenting propaganda and turn toward your own good parenting instincts. Of course, educating ourselves about parenting is essential—I've memorized parts of Sears's *Baby Book* after looking up fevers or rashes at 3 A.M. more than a dozen times—but your own internal voice can often be your best guide.

It's a requirement of parenting and marriage to constantly strive to be the best person you can be, and this means investing in your own psychological growth. Instead of acquiring parenting skills like potatoes in a burlap sack, focus on personal attributes, such as compassion, psychological understanding, and emotional depth. Ronald Levant, in *Masculinity Reconstructed,* defines the new skills required of fathers: "Becoming the kind of father a man's family now needs him to be is a huge challenge. The best way for men to meet that challenge is by putting some effort into developing the skills that I call emotional intelligence—emotional self-awareness, emotional expressiveness, and emotional empathy. . . . The more he's worked free of

What Equal Parents Can Give Children

When you find your family or your child in crisis, either mini or major, regroup as a couple. Family trauma can severely strain a marriage, fracturing couples. Staying connected and in sync is critical to supporting your child and family in the best possible way. What will serve your child best? Should you research on the Internet, go to outside resources, or just sit and listen? Practice family teamwork to develop a strategy to support your child.

- Be calm, loving, and consistent.
- Stay connected with each other and your child.
- Focus on what's important: loving each other and your child.
- Don't hesitate to use outside resources.
- Listen.

Parenting School

Parenting often requires outside help and resources, and as equal parents it helps if you're both committed to information gathering. If the village elders aren't nearby when you need them, take to the streets, or the Web for word-of-mouth parenting advice.

- Friends: You should each have access to a few great parents as resources.
- Lectures: Make sure you both attend local parenting lectures at your library, school, or other community center.
- Books: When was the last time you both read a relationship or parenting book and discussed the different methods or philosophies to see if they rang true for you?
- Web sites: Do you know the popular Web site to get home remedies, advice, or information?

the traditional masculine belief that a man must sacrifice himself to his job, the more he'll be available to his wife and children." Highly developed emotional intelligence gives you the broad stroke perspective that is constantly needed in parenting: It helps you understand your child's emotional reality, experiences, and struggles in a light that's theirs alone and not colored with your own childhood baggage.

When you're confronted with an "issue"—a son who hates school, a daughter with severe separation anxiety, a child grappling with the hard job of growing up—as a parent, you are apt to want to "fix" the problem. Just as you can put antibiotic ointment and a Band-Aid on a knee and kiss away the tears, you want to solve the emotional hurts of your children. And when you can, you must do so together as parents. You might indeed find the answers in books, and you're likely to also find other answers in your hearts. Both parents' loving attentiveness, practiced together, speaks loudly to your children: We love you, we're right here standing by you.

Final Step: State Your Parenting and Child Care Intentions and Goals

The responsibility for the care of children lies with both parents—and it is vital to equal parenting that partners mutually agree upon and determine what's best for their family and child. Just as you have goals for yourselves or your careers—like New Year's resolutions or making partner by age 35—stating your parenting intentions is the first step toward making them come true.

When I first voiced the idea of changing parenting roles with my husband, it was met with resistance and uncertainty. How could we possibly make this work? How would we pay our bills? What employers might support a flexible work arrangement? Was I giving an ultimatum or threatening Gill's career momentum? Once we realized that we both had the same goal—to love our kids in the best possible way and spend quality time with them while still maintaining an exterior life—a truce was called. Gill realized that he wanted desperately to spend more time with our children, and I realized that I needed to have more contact with the outside world. We were on the same family team. Neither of us wanted to negate the other's parenting roles, nor did we want to clip each other's wings and prohibit our growth in the outside world.

A Husband's Viewpoint

The Best Things about Parenting Full-Time

1. Not missing out on my children's lives!

2. Unconditional love, all the time

3. A heart more open

4. Gratefulness for experience—and time—with kids

5. Perspective: everything else seems less important than loving my kids

The Most Difficult Things about Parenting Full-Time

1. Shifting part or all of my time to unpaid work

2. Isolation, hard to find other fathers

3. Letting go of past breadwinning role

4. Fear of losing future earning power

5. Floors! Keeping them clean . . .

We knew equal parenting wouldn't happen when I was pregnant (with our second child), but we knew we wanted it to happen in the future, and many of our day-to-day decisions were made keeping our parenting intention in mind. For instance, instead of the more expensive car we might have chosen in the past, we bought a hybrid gas-electric car, because the monthly payment fit our budget and would lower our insurance and gas bill. We consciously made an economic decision that would move us closer to our desired parenting dynamic.

Stating your intention—for both of you to share in parenting and work—gives you a baseline from which to work. Most parents have vague ideas of how they want to parent—and with fluctuating work and economic environments, it can be hard to pin down specifics. Communicating these ideas is important, even if it's articulating what you *don't* want. Betsy, a hospital labor worker says, "Before we had Lauren, I made it very clear that I did not want to be in the situation that many of my friends are—their husbands are gone 12 hours a day and see their kids only on the weekends. I alone did not want to be responsible for raising a baby. My husband expressed genuine commitment about sharing the parenting role. He had seen too many friends miss out on their kids' early years. I guess this is one advantage of waiting until 'later' to have a child. We hadn't worked out details of who would do what on a day-to-day basis, but it was clear that we would both work and we would both take care of Lauren. In fact, in anticipation of Lauren's arrival, he quit his incredibly time-intensive job and found something much closer to home and less demanding."

Another woman, Tara, who was in school when she and her boyfriend got pregnant, explained, "It was an unplanned pregnancy, but once we found out, we knew we wanted to practice 'attachment parenting' and create a home with one full-time stay-at-home parent and the other a part-time worker. We have a lot of family close by, so everyone was very supportive—no one is letting us starve. I plan to go back to school once our child is in kindergarten, but for now we both want to be available." She and her husband are committed to caring for their child with little day care, and also to sending Tara back to school to finish her education. They are in agreement about what's

Creating Intention Statements

Depending on where you are in your parenting cycle, state your intentions about what you both want today. If you disagree, talk through to a compromise. Here are some suggestions to get you started.

● With young children, our ideal parenting scenario would be _____

_____.

● We would like to put our children in _____ hours of weekly child care, in a child care environment like _____

_____.

● As our children grow, we would like to change/maintain/trade our parenting roles by _____

_____.

● We want to combine work and family balance by _____

_____.

● We would like our after-school care to be _____

_____.

important to them and for their child and committed to following through with their intentions and goals.

Being in harmony about your child care plans may take negotiating, financial planning, and compromising. You may need to put off school or turn down the promotion and job that requires more travel, or you may be required to work more for financial reasons instead of being home with your children. Your desires and intentions will change over the years, probably as often as the seasons. Stay-at-home parents might be begging to work after a few years, and those working long, pressure-filled or mind-numbing hours may yearn to be home with their children. Keep your eye on the prize—loving your children—and let your intention statement inform your decisions.

NEGOTIATION POINTS

Negotiating the tasks of making a dentist appointments, or carpooling to the dance may seem trivial, but such matters, day in and day out, make up the life of a parent. Negotiating helps you keep these tasks from taking on a force of their own: usually in ugly words such as "he never . . ." or "she never . . ." It assumes that your children are, in fact, *your* children. You share in taking care of them just as you share in loving them.

The Negotiation Points in this chapter will help you start to define and assign responsibility for the work of parenting.

Everyday Tasks are nonstop, such as meals and child care.

Ongoing Tasks include frequent, but not daily tasks, such as doctor's appointments or helping with homework.

Special Tasks are those that happen the least, such as cleaning out a closet or attending a school meeting.

With the lists below, you can begin identifying who is now doing these tasks. For some tasks, you might have help, such as a family member, nanny, or child care center—and you can determine together how to build a supportive environment using that help. But you may also see if there are imbalances or areas that are sorely neglected due to lack of support or time resources. This is where negotiations and agreements are in order.

Task	Everyday	Ongoing	Special
Child Care and Schooling			
Young Children			
Child care management			
Interviewing care providers			
Researching preschools			
Filling out applications to preschool or day care			
Getting doctor/immunization records for school			
Summer camps			
Communication between care provider and family			
School-Aged Children			
Researching schools			
Applying to schools; managing application process			
Getting doctor/ immunization records			
School pickup and drop-off			
PTA and teacher meetings			
Volunteer hours at school			
Fund-raisers			
Arranging after-school care			
Helping with homework			
Helping with school supplies			
Health Maintenance			
Make doctor appointments			
Make dentist appointments			
Well doctor visits			
Dental exams			

Task	Everyday	Ongoing	Special
Sick doctor visits			
Sick days home from school or day care			
Preventative care			
Alternative health treatments			
Researching health issues			
Haircuts			
Clothing			
Buying clothes			
Taking children shopping for special occasions			
Sorting through outgrown clothes			
Changing summer to winter wardrobes			
Organizing children's drawers and closet space			
Food			
Organizing baby-food needs			
Packing food for child care			
Packing school lunches			
After-school snacks			
Teaching children about healthy eating			
Preparing meals together			
Activities			
Children's birthday party planning			
Field trips, outings			
Reading			
Signing up for classes			

Task	Everyday	Ongoing	Special
Teaching activities, such as sports, music, science			
Attending classes with child (drop-off/pickup)			
Teaching children how to help with cleanup			
Social life			
Planning playdates			
Weekend birthday party attendance			
Planning weekend activities for family			
Organization			
Going through old toys			
Organizing children's room			
Cleaning children's room			

INTENTION: COMMIT TO INTENTIONAL PARENTING ROLES

Pablo had wanted to speak to me even though he wasn't yet a parent. A landscaper with well-worn work-boots that he took off before he came inside my home, he described himself as "a guy in recovery for a decade" who had a miserable, traumatic childhood. His greatest wish was for he and his wife to grow a loving, stable family—and because of his recovery efforts and honesty, he was clearly going to succeed. "I don't have children yet—we're working on that—but the thing I want to be more than anything in this world is a good father to my kids and a loyal husband to my wife." Pablo had a sweetness to him that was vulnerable and strong. "My wife and I are both in Alcoholics Anonymous," he explained, "and we decided we wanted our 5-year chip before we start a family—and we only have 1 more year to go. We have also gone to counseling so that we can work on erasing our bad family history and not repeat it." Pablo outlined their financial preparations: "We're hard-working, but we don't want to work all the time when we have a family. We both feel that working part-time, maybe my wife 3 days a week and me 4 days, is the ideal we'd like to shoot for." For 3 years, they had been saving money to buy a home or to supplement their income when they became parents.

Few people give such foresight to parenting roles years in advance of becoming parents. Pablo's efforts were formidable, and his scrupulous intention reflected his genuine desire to overcome his childhood history. Often, in the midst of our parenting years, our intentions suddenly shift. Candy, a retail-store manager, married to her second husband, raising three combined children, said, "I was surprised that when my kids became teenagers, we felt someone needed to be home even more. I thought at that age I would feel more freedom to work, but instead I found that we needed to be monitoring and participating in our children's lives at this emotional and vulnerable time." While their kids where younger, she and her husband had both worked full-time to make ends meet, yet their children were excelling in school and at home at this time. As the children grew older, things changed, though: "We needed to know what they were doing after school, who they were seeing, who they were dating, was their school work getting done." Both agreed that they needed to revisit their parenting intentions again, and as a result, they altered their working lives.

Defining your parenting roles is an ongoing process, before your child is born and during their lifetimes. Recently, neighbors of ours were practicing what they thought of as "tough love" with their 29-year-old son, who was committed to being a musician and living in their home without paying rent. They were equally committed to encouraging his independence and fostering his self-confidence by pushing him out the door. The role of parent is for life. You are always making choices about how you want to parent, no matter what age your children might be.

Raising the Children Intention Statement:

We commit to intentionally designing our parenting roles and being equally responsible for child care and child-related tasks.

_____   _____
Signed   Signed

CHAPTER 6

Taking Care of Home and Hearth

"Keeping house has always encompassed knowing and doing whatever is needed to make the home a small, living society with the capacities to meet the needs of people in their private life: everything from meals, shelter, clothing, warmth, and other physical necessities to books and magazines, music, play . . . and much more."

–Cheryl Mendelson, *Home Comforts*

Christa sat on my couch dressed in slacks and a sweater, poised and friendly. A stay-at-home mother of two and former marketing executive, she expressed herself clearly and confidently, "I want to give my kids a stay-at-home mother, because that's what I had. And when it comes to taking care of them and the household, I think I just do a better job." Slowly her history emerged: Christa sacrificed a career she loved, because she felt it was her duty to stay home—and because she believes she can keep the house cleaner than her husband can—"I know how to clean a counter better than he does," she said matter-of-factly, adding, "I don't think he even knows where the vacuum cleaner is." Meanwhile, her husband—who professes to be a "homebody"—has taken on an extra shift to pay the bills and is now missing his children as he works 6 days a week. Christa will not consider working part-time in order to share the financial responsibility with her husband and allow him to be more involved in family life again. She bristled: "I feel like it's my responsibility, as the mom, to take care of them and the home." When I asked her whether working part-time might benefit their family finances, but also might give her personal fulfillment, she rolled her eyes slightly annoyed, explaining that the household would fall apart. "My mother stayed home and loved her life as a mother and housewife. I think I can too."

As Christa's story illustrates, many of us still believe that it's a woman's job to take care of home and hearth, an idea reaffirmed by every TV commercial depicting a woman embracing a toilet brush as if she just won an Oscar. But cleaning house is not an innate ability. Women are not genetically coded with cleaning finesse superior to men's. We do not fold towels better, scrub toilets harder, or prepare better dinners because we're equipped with ovaries. We have been taught and socialized to be more responsive to needs in the home. Simply put, we have had more practice. Christa is like many of us as she negates her husband's ability to clean and also rebuffs his offer to share responsibility: Even if he wants to help, he can't do it right. It becomes a vicious circle.

Some of us are just afraid to ask for help around the house; we don't want to provoke an argument that might not end quickly. Yet housework is the topic that exasperates women and gives ammunition to arguments in households everywhere. This chapter will give you creative ideas and solutions that will make everyone—the cleaner and noncleaner, the organized and disheveled—understand expectations and find a comfortable land of truce and compromise. For those with husbands who are ready and willing to take on a fair share of housework, this chapter will provide the structure for defining and negotiating your roles. A word of caution: The issue of housework and family culture will not sail quietly into the night. And each time we laugh or act righteously at men's supposed ineptitude around the house, we only increase the likelihood that we will be the ones left holding the dustpan.

THERE'S NO PLACE LIKE HOME

Creating a healthy, vibrant household environment is one of the most essential aspects of parenting. Running the household may seem mundane when you look at the nitty-gritty of standalone tasks such as folding underwear and organizing the pantry—but creating the home life and nest for your family is profoundly far-reaching. We cherish expressions like "there's no place like home," "home is where the heart is," and "home sweet home" precisely because we know how true they are.

A home is an emotional sanctuary, providing us with love and support, as Clare Cooper Marcus writes, "A home fulfills many needs: a place of self-expression, a vessel of memories, a refuge from the outside world, a cocoon where we can feel nurtured and let down our guard." Through family interaction, creative activity, and personal exploration we make up our unique family culture. We read, we participate, we touch, we eat. Books, movies, playdough, food. It's in our homes that many discoveries are made—the quiet pleasure of reading, the mystery of an ant colony in a jar, the joy of joke-telling with siblings. At its best, the structure of home—both emotional and intellectual supports—gives us the bedrock we need to build our lives.

When we look back upon our own family and childhood, it's the feelings of home that make up our strongest impressions. I remember the hot metallic smell of the waffle iron on a Sunday morning, listening to Fleetwood Mac, and overeating waffles. I love pomegranate jelly, because my grandmother and mother made this every year, a rich, time-intensive family tradition. My husband reminisces about long days spent on boats; a tight-knit, loyal group of family and

The Housework Quiz

You may think you do it all, and you may truly do it all. In most couples, the wives underestimate their housework contribution, and the husbands overestimate theirs. Below is a short quiz to determine who is the true domestic dominator.

1. Where are the mop, the children's Tylenol, and emergency numbers for the babysitter?
2. What kind of cleaner does your family use on the toilet? In the kitchen?
3. What is the difference between a number 2 and number 5 plastic for recycling?
4. When is the car due for an oil change?
5. In which drawer do the kids keep their bathing suits?
6. Without looking, how much laundry detergent, dishwashing liquid, and milk do you have in the house?
7. What month do you prune roses? Put snow tires on the car?
8. Where is the best place to buy fish, meat, bread, and the cheapest toilet paper?
9. Name three meals you can make in 5 minutes.

Quick Tips

Housework is the favorite complaint of women and the dreaded subject of men. But that doesn't always hold true. If you need immediate relief, try the tips below.

1. Discuss "How Do You Feel about Housework" on page 201.
2. Go over the communication techniques in "The Ground Rules: Talking about Housework" on page 205.
3. Define your Family Standard of Cleanliness (see "Step One: Define Your Standards" on page 208).
4. Now, what are your top three problem areas? Find solutions, step by step.

friends; and the Chinese Bed, a large and elaborate canopied bed from Hong Kong that was frequently the site of forts, slumber parties, and roughhousing. It is moments like these from our childhood, from planting radishes in a garden, putting gold stars on our chore list, or the yellow and green paint from our first bedroom, that informs us who we are as adults, parents, and spouses and contributes to a new vision of home.

There are also the things we may have yearned for in our childhood, such as family vacations, a refrigerator stocked with food, socializing with other families in the community, or a lawn to run barefoot on—things that we did not have in our families that as adults we may equate with a happy, rich home environment. A childhood friend I spent time with after school was mortified that his family's kitchen was always a mess—and to this day I know it's deeply important for him to have a clean, tidy home. I, on the other hand, thought a messy kitchen was crazy and liberating. I admired his mother for working outside of the home, and even as a grade-school-age kid, I felt there was something intriguing about his mother, a teacher who entertained us with stories of her classroom. Each of us, though, has our own needs—met and unmet—and impressions, good and bad. A messy house is liberating to one and oppressive to another. As adults, we have the great opportunity to create a family home environment that fulfills our needs and our children's needs now and for a lifetime.

Where Our Hearts Lie

I'm always striving to create a rich home environment, especially around the holidays. I want my family home to exude love, warmth, mouthwatering aromas, compassion, health—you name it. Usually though, December leaves me feeling like Sisyphus, forever pushing the boulder up the hill, strong and enduring, yet ineffective and hopeless. One year, while I was our family's primary caregiver, Matthew had a 2-month long ear infection that three rounds of antibiotics could not cure, and Ella had a cold and cough that would not quit. A common cold is one thing, but secondary infections for young children often mean that life as we know it must stop: I could not work; I got little sleep; I became head nurse, administering various potions, vitamins, and medicine.

The weeks became a series of appointments: I saw our pediatrician, our beloved homeopathic practitioner, the chiropractor, and even an intuitive healer in my desperation to get my kids healthy. I noticed with dismay (and not missing the cruel irony) that, while os-

tensibly writing a book on equal parenting, I traveled to various doctors 18 times (but who's counting?), and Gill went, let me see if I can
add them up. Oh yeah, zero. Our family life went temporarily hay-
wire. In the month when I had the most extra things to do, I wasn't
able to handle the basics, and it showed: Mail went unopened, the car
became a mini recycling center for old toys, clothes, and papers, and
my house sank into a depressing, impossible mess.

Meanwhile, my dreams for a holiday home had to shift to fit reality. Other people's homes filled with decorations, family, and smells
of freshly baked gingerbread. I couldn't tackle all that, and luckily I
didn't try. But I also refused to give up entirely, and, little by little,
I could feel some measure of holiday spirit return to our family: I
went to a latke party with girlfriends. Our family attended a Christmas
musical celebration. Ella and I made holiday cookies with little girls
and their mothers. We appreciated the richness of family, friends, and
peace in our neighborhood—and focused on all we had. Slowly our
home went from a small disaster site to one with pockets of Christmas
cheer.

In the 2 days of Christmas celebrations, we were surrounded by
family, cousins, and in-laws. Our home was loud with the sounds of
children playing, sisters and brothers laughing, and parents and grandparents adoring their children. We cuddled on the couch, we warmed
our toes by the fire, the adults drank decadent whipped cream eggnog
with a touch of bourbon, and we ate food that brought us to the table
together in gratitude.

The month leading up to the holidays may be cluttered and difficult. We may fall woefully short of our ideals for holiday trappings. It's
actually no different than during the rest of the year, when our house

Your Family Culture

Talk about the physical environment and family culture you want to create in your home. What qualities and activities or experiences do you want represented; what's currently working and not working so well?

- What are the favorite elements from your childhood home?
- What are the most important qualities in your home now—and what is missing?
- How would you like your children to feel in their home?
- What kind of family culture is important to you?
- What type of "open door" policy—with family and friends—feels comfortable?

Words to think about: tranquil, private, welcoming, creative chaos, cosmopolitan, vibrant, orderly, learning, safe, respectful, spiritual, meditative, structured, scheduled and soon.

Ideas to think about: sports, music, books and magazines, composting and gardening, recycling, nature, art, science, computers, socializing, neighbors, family tradition, religious practice, volunteerism, and hobbies.

If your list includes qualities or ideas not represented in your home, think about what steps you can take to make it happen. For "welcoming," maybe you'd like to host a neighborhood party or encourage your children to invite friends over more frequently. For "science," maybe you could plan some nature hikes, visit a local science museum or animal rescue, or check out books at the library on a topic that interests the family. Make a list of the words and their corresponding action steps as you put together your House, Family, and Community Goals using the worksheet beginning on page 223.

may not look exactly in the condition we wish it would. But in the end, our homes remain a living and breathing embodiment of our family love, providing us with shelter and safety to express our love to each other during holidays and every other day of the year.

HOW ARE WE STRUGGLING?

Our homes are the most popular battleground for hurling complaints and accusations and finding fault. Quite simply, we are struggling with the fact that women do more housework and child-related tasks than men do. The mixed bag of tedium and monotony that is part and parcel of home management can zap our energy and fuel resentment. Women and men at home may crave more mental stimulation, more creativity, or a paycheck. Self-esteem can be hard to come by when folding laundry and organizing the sock drawer.

Sascha, a warm and outgoing woman with two children, discussed her relationship in one of my interview groups: "I think we all agree that we have loving, intelligent, good husbands or partners. It's the boring, mundane minutia of housework that is the crux of the complaints. . . . I want it to be second nature for Bob to take the dirty water glass when he's walking from the living room to the kitchen. I want him to notice that glass, feel motivated to bring it to the kitchen, and as he's walking from the living room to the kitchen, pick up a jacket or a book and put that in its proper place, too. Just as part of walking. What is missing is simple awareness, though, and it drives me absolutely nuts!"

The issue of awareness and mental responsibility dominated conversations I had with women. Many had husbands who were more than happy to help out around the house as long as they were given specific and ongoing direction. "Please keep the laundry going. Can you get the clothes to Good Will on Sacramento Street at 10 this morning? Honey, sort the Leaning Tower of Mail on the dining room table." According to most women, their husbands exhibited a severe lack of awareness of what was happening in the home, sometimes because the men were working most of the day, and other times because they could rely on their wives to take charge and had relinquished responsibility in total. For example, my husband went to the grocery store on his way home from work. He came home with four bags of food, but not milk, eggs, diapers, or toilet paper—all crucial items we were out of. "Did you not notice that we're using paper towels in the bathroom and haven't had milk for coffee or cereal?" I asked accusatorily. It was hard for me to understand how he wasn't aware of this. After all, I had been keeping the shopping list of all we needed— taking mental responsibility for noticing what we needed, writing it down, and prioritizing a trip to the store. I was grateful that he went to the store, especially without being asked, but I was irritated that I was the one who noticed everything we needed and that he hadn't asked me for a list. Sure, I was home more than he, but he used toilet paper, too, and his morning coffee had been sorely lacking in milk.

Developing awareness and mental responsibility may be a matter of following the steps in this chapter. It may also require a major personality paradigm shift that takes years to fully develop. As they say, though, awareness is the first step. So awareness of awareness, for you and your partner, is the first step toward sharing family household responsibility.

THE END OF SUZIE HOMEMAKER: GENDER ROLES AND HOME MANAGEMENT

Betty Crocker, Mrs. Paul's Fish Sticks, Amy's Organic Frozen Dinners, Annie's Organic Macaroni and Cheese. John Deere Tractors, Lawn Boy mowers, Benjamin Moore house paint. Even the most mundane of products insidiously reinforce the notion of division of household labor. And for generations, women and men have accepted their ordained roles in and around the home. Most of us have a mental picture of our mothers in the kitchen making dinner. Fathers worked outside the home, they did yard work, and they barbequed. Even when mothers worked outside the home, they generally remained responsible for the care and nourishment of the family and the family home. Marilyn Yalom, in *A History of the Wife,* describes the 1950s and -60s: "Gender roles were clear-cut: Men were expected to be 'good providers' and women to be full-time wives and mothers. For the most part, the men did not want their wives to work outside the home, since it reflected badly on the husband's earning power. He, in turn, considered it inappropriate to pitch into housekeeping once he came home from work. In about four-fifths of the families, cooking, laundry, and cleaning were exclusively female occupations."

Times have changed, yet many of us still hold onto the image of what a mother and father are supposed to do in the home. The past 20 years have clearly seen men begin to contribute more to the homemaker role as their wives have entered the workforce, but the disparity between who does the housework, even between couples who work comparable hours, is dramatic. Typically, men contribute to yard work and home maintenance, while women carry 75 percent or more of the burden for grocery shopping, cooking, cleaning, laundry, and dishwashing. The difference is that the men's tasks can be delayed, often for weeks and months, while women's tasks are daily and constant. Couples in traditional and nontraditional parenting arrangements are in deadlock. It's a power struggle and an identity crisis wrestling with the tradition—and steady resistance of—gender-assigned roles.

In one of my interview groups women expressed resentment yet acquiescence. One stay-at-home mom says of her husband, "I barely let him enter the kitchen. I think he intentionally makes a huge mess just to get out of cooking." Her friend follows, "Before we had kids, we both worked all the time, and I did maybe 70 percent of all the housework and meals. Now that we have kids, it's even worse." The full-time working mom sums up what the group concludes: "Let's face it. Whether you're with the kids all day or working at a job, women end up doing most of it. It's hopeless."

Even in marriages that have chosen to have a stay-at-home parent, the pressure is on: Quincy, with two children under age three, explains, "I take care of the kids and house all day, and when my husband gets home from work, he thinks he's 'off.' I get to hear about how he works hard all day and deserves to put his feet up and relax. Meanwhile, I'm feeding the kids, getting them bathed and to bed, doing laundry, and picking up the house. And then I'm up half the night settling and resettling the children! My husband may work hard for 10 or 12 hours a day, but I work around the clock." Both Quincy and her husband explain that they have chosen a traditional marriage arrangement, because they think it's best for families and children. When Quincy ventures that this is not exactly the role she signed up for, her husband remarks, "You women have it easy." In Quincy's situation, because she doesn't have a quantifiable monetary value to her

How Do You Feel about Housework?

Have an honest conversation with yourself and your partner about where things stand. Some of us are furious that our husbands can just sit and watch television without folding laundry at the same time. Others are grateful that our husbands share equal or more responsibility.

- Do you have pent-up resentment about housework?
- What are the areas that are most upsetting to you?
- Are you afraid of being confined to any housework roles because of your parents' model?
- How do you feel about your home in general?
- What do you like about housework?

husband, as mother and housewife she feels timid and sometimes even powerless when making decisions about purchases, vacations, and her own personal freedoms.

THE EQUAL PARENTING AGREEMENT TO TAKE CARE OF HOME AND HEARTH

We commit to being equally responsible for finding solutions that support a healthy, loving family environment.

This chapter may be the most difficult or contentious for you to work through, but may provide relief and inspire great teamwork in your partnership. Taking care of home and hearth involves feeding the family and running the household, plus the organization and planning it takes to maintain your family culture. It includes planning holiday celebrations, managing the oil change on the car, and writing thank you notes. It means knowing when you're out of laundry detergent, which one to buy that doesn't give your daughter a rash, and who to call to fix the clogged drain. In sum, it's not only what must be done, but also what we would like to do to maintain a loving home.

Working through the steps, exercises, and negotiation points in this chapter, you can design your own home life. What role does nutrition and cooking play in your family? How can you maintain safe vehicles and a secure home? Would you like to be a part of your community? Volunteer in the school? How will you celebrate birthdays and holidays? Answering these questions will provide a road map. Then you can decide how to navigate.

Chances are you may not have a relationship in which it's possible or practical to divide the housekeeping and family maintenance work equally. But it is important to tackle the challenge of doing these things as a problem in which you will both find a solution. Figuring out how your home will stay healthy and happy shows that you are in this together. You are emotionally committed to the relationship and equal partners in solving problems. Just as you make career or job decisions by consulting each other, you should manage the family culture and house together, even if one person is primarily responsible. In this way, it's not devalued. A husband is not saying, "It's not worth my time to clean the toilet bowl," but instead saying, "How can we keep our bathroom clean, respecting each other's time availability and contributing fairly?" Instead of saying "Just tell me what to do, and I'll do it," it's committing to a higher level of awareness and being responsible for noticing what needs cleaning or what is needed from the grocery store. It's taking on the mental responsibility and accountability for the many unseen and invisible tasks, as well as the daily chores.

The payoff of sharing household responsibility is huge. So explains Scott Coltrane, professor of sociology at UC Irvine, in his astute book *Family Man*: "When men do take on more of the mundane domestic tasks of cooking, cleaning, and child-tending, however, the balance of power in a household begins to shift. If husbands assume a larger share of the housework, employed wives escape total responsibility for the second shift, and women enjoy better mental health. In addition, when fathers take on significant responsibility for children, they begin to develop sensitivities that have been assumed to come with being a mother. When fathers share in routine parenting, children thrive intellectually and emotionally, and they grow up with less rigid gender stereotypes. Sharing household labor thus carries the potential for transforming the meaning of gender in this and future generations. Perhaps more importantly, if men took responsibility for family work and performed more of the everyday tasks that it takes to run a household, there are strong indications that gender inequality and discrimination against women would decrease substantially."

Before You Begin: Letting Go of Perfection

I rang the doorbell of a home with lush flowerbeds, immaculate landscaping, and swept walkways. My interview subject, a pretty woman dressed in a chic outfit with simple makeup, answered the door. Audrey welcomed me into a house that was spare and elegant. Our interview was short. She explained in precise language that her marriage was wonderful, her child was a dream, her job was quite excellent, and her husband was smart and successful. I drove away admiring her home and her poise but left wondering whom it was I had just spoken with. She hadn't revealed anything about the experiences of mother-hood and marriage or shared emotional truths of the tender and dif-ficult moments. I regretted that she had not trusted me enough to reveal her inner life—and felt compassion for the pressures she must feel to present to the world a perfect self.

Even if you've long since given up on living in a Martha Stewart–perfect world, there is still pressure to strive for it. We all have areas of vulnerability, and our home lives are particularly fertile grounds for insecurity. We're afraid of people seeing our messy house or knowing that we suffer from emotional lows or that our marriage isn't perfect. Often the idea of "keeping up appearances" takes on a life of its own. One woman explained that financial problems were forcing her family to dramatically change their lifestyle, and her hus-band felt shame about sharing the news with friends. Once they could no longer keep it a secret, the outpouring of support surprised them: "It wasn't that people supported us with money. That was not the point. People shared with us their hardships, financial and otherwise, and let us know they were there for us. We felt so close to so many families, and we were reminded why we chose to have these people in our lives in the first place."

It's our personal stories that make us human and real—and our homes reflect our individuality and family culture. My friend Emily has an immaculate, lovely home. No cobwebs, up-to-the-minute framed pictures of the kids, mail put in its proper place, tasteful art-work in all the rooms, and few telltale signs of the messes that come with children. I am in awe of her house and appreciate that Emily takes great pride in having a beautiful home. My house has piles. Piles of laundry. Piles of mail. Piles of school forms, books, magazines, videos. My desk is a visual interpretation of the Tower of Babel. I frequently sigh with resignation, because I crave orderliness and clean surfaces—but this is the home we have made to nest our family now, priorities loosely in place, crumbs and all. The dirt on the children's clothes show how hard they played at the park, and the finger paint on the wall reminds us of a child's creativity. A botched Thanksgiving turkey, the thank-you notes that never got written or the birth announcements that were never sent, although not ideal, are just stuff. Without the trip-ups we couldn't enjoy the triumphs. Let go of the race for perfection and embrace the stage of life you are in now. What really matters is in your heart.

The Ground Rules: Talking about Housework

Communicating about housework can turn into a tit-for-tat session, usually ending in hurt feelings, defensiveness, and "Have you ever once mopped the kitchen floor?" or "When did you ever balance a checkbook?"-type accusations. In truth, we all have areas that we neglect while secretly hoping our partner will pick up the slack. It's important that we find ways to discuss household chores and family responsibilities without it turning into a face-off of pit bulls.

There are many communication tips scattered throughout this book, but there are a few particular to the chore wars that are worth noting.

Start a request on a positive note. A stockbroker mom, whose husband is the primary parent, says her husband is a pro at this: "He tells me what a great mother I am, which is always nice to hear, and then he'll ask if it's a good time to discuss something. I usually panic a bit, but because I know he's coming from a loving place, I'm not so reactionary. He'll say something like, 'It upsets me that the car is so dirty all the time and that it doesn't feel like it's important to you to keep it clean. I'd like to make it a priority, so how can we work on this?'"

Timing can be the difference between a loving, constructive exchange and a battle royal. The worst time to bring up for the umpteenth time how the toilet seat is always left up or to point out the new stain on the couch is when you're steamed. Remember, too, that everyday events can be stressful—such as being stuck in a traffic jam or the arrival of your mother-in-law from out of town—and are also not the best times to bring up sensitive and important issues. I'm an expert at wanting to discuss bill-paying as my husband is nodding off for the night. Bad idea. Leave it for another time, in a few hours or days, when you're not transferring all of your relationship problems into one little issue and are instead treating it for what it is. Just a toilet seat. Just a couch. Not the end of the world.

Pick your battles. When you focus on nitpicky things, like not hanging wet towels up correctly, it's often a sign that something else in your relationship is out of whack. My loving, devoted husband is the towel culprit, and no matter how many times I ask him, he is apparently unable to spread a wet towel out on the rack so it will dry. When we're totally in sync in our relationship, I couldn't care less about this and am happy to wander into the bathroom and fix the towels. He is a generous, hard-working, supportive man, and if his biggest flaw is the towels, then so be it. When I'm unhappy about something in our relationship, though, the towel issue becomes very, very big. "Why can't he just hang up the damn towel?" It's a red flag to me that something bigger and deeper is going on between us.

Double-check the message. Often we are sending a message that we didn't intend to send. When I come home from a business dinner, I walk into the house and start quizzing Gill about the kids, phone messages, and household chores. I forget to greet him lovingly, and he doesn't feel my appreciation for the sweet care he gives our children. When we forget to say the kind words and appreciate their efforts, it hits our partners hard. As Pete, an arborist and father of two children describes: "I get the kids ready for school one or two mornings a week. My wife works part-time, so usually she's the one handling the morning routine. When it's my turn, though, I love it, even though it's difficult and chaotic, and I don't do it frequently enough to be a pro. Inevitably, I do something 'wrong.' I give my son the wrong food in his lunch, I'm a few minutes late to school, or I forget to make somebody wear a jacket. . . . No matter what I do, it seems that I'm getting in trouble for how I do it. I really do understand that my wife would like me to be more conscious of the messes and nutrition and brushing teeth, and I am improving all the time, but I'm not appreciated at all for what I am doing—and it makes me feel like 'What's the use?'" So, remember to send loving and appreciative messages—the messages that we in fact prefer to receive.

INTENTIONAL STEPS TOWARD MAKING A COMFORTABLE HOME

Think of housework as meditation, and the steps, exercises, and negotiation points that follow as the beginning of searching your soul to explore home and hearth and what works for your family, your relationship, and you.

Step One: Define Your Standards

Before we had children I did almost everything. My husband says it's because my standard of cleanliness was higher than his. That's why it never occurred to him to sweep the floor. "So you want to live in a pigsty," I'd say, "We would have to get to that point before you would clean?"

—Xu, doctor and mother of two

I don't trust my husband to do the laundry. We have very different standards. I'm always thinking about what needs to be done. That's sort of my whole reality. I go around ticking all of the time. And for Rob, the house could be falling apart—this is an exaggeration—but he's down there singing the blues, having a great old time. And he'll say, "I'm a passionate person." That's sort of his reasoning. Just different standards.

—Lori, sales rep and mother of one

Like Xu and Lori, women everywhere explain, "His standard of cleanliness is just not up to mine," while men have rebutted with, "She has such high standards, it's not even dirty when she says it's dirty." It is the second most predictable item I hear in my interviews, right after "Men can't multitask." Perhaps women have become confused from the cleaning fumes. How else to explain why women have bought into the argument that our standards of cleanliness are just unreasonably high? So for those of you not living with Felix Unger let me spell it out: It is not an unreasonably high standard to expect the bathroom to be scrubbed more frequently than on the Winter Solstice. Nor is it crazy to want to be able to see the linoleum of your kitchen floor. And it's certainly not beyond the pale to want clean sheets for the New Year.

Just because people may choose not to see the dirt does not mean that it's not there and that it shouldn't be taken care of.

It is unreasonable, however, to expect perfection, which is why agreeing on your Family Standard of Cleanliness (FSOC) may save you approximately 642 arguments in the course of your marriage. Besides, wouldn't you rather be arguing over things more exciting than laundry and toilet bowls and instead discussing politics, global warming, and your crazy relatives? Your FSOC is the attainable and negotiated goal you have for your home. For example, in my family, our standard regarding dishes is that we do not do dishes immediately after dinner, but we will generally get them done before we go to bed. Our time with our children and with each other is so short that we don't want the dishes to sabotage talking with each other or interrupt our enjoyment of bath and story time with our kids. Our agreement is that the kitchen will get cleaned, but there's no rush. The dishes will wait for us, ever so patiently. Other families might feel completely different: They might not be able to enjoy this time *until* the dishes are done.

This is the beauty of devising your own FSOC. It's unique to your family. As you discuss what's important to you, keep in mind that it's not a discussion of who will do what, but a mutually agreed-upon ideal standard of cleanliness for your home. You are not trying to define the bottom-of-the-barrel standard of slovenliness that you can degenerate into or the white-glove-test standard of perfection that you secretly or not-so-secretly aspire to. Be honest with yourself and with each other about the most important things for you in your home, what you can live with, and what drives you crazy. In a rational discussion, it's hard to argue against a certain amount of cleanliness and also hard to lobby for total sanitary perfection. If you are not in com-

Defining Your Family Standard of Cleanliness

Here are some of the main areas of your home to consider. Remember that this is a practical, realistic goal of how we would like our home to look and feel.

Kitchen	Laundry
Living room or common area	Entryway
Children's bedroom(s)	Garage
Bathroom(s)	Yard
Parent's bedroom	

Here are examples of our Family Standard of Cleanliness (FSOC).

* We keep our bathroom picked up—toiletries, clothes, and bath toys—and the towels are hung up to dry. The bathroom is not spotless, but it's not cluttered. We have a housecleaner come every 2 weeks to do the nitty-gritty.

* Our living room is our Grand Central Station. We try our best to pick up the day's worth of accumulated newspapers, toys, and clothes, but sometimes this room will be a mess. And this is okay.

plete agreement about your family standard of cleanliness, you both need to expand your comfort zone. You must compromise. If you are the neat freak who is constantly battling the slobs of the house, it's time to mellow out and define a standard that is attainable. And if you're the slob of the house, it's time get on your hands and knees and clean the corner behind the bathroom door.

Step Two: Throw Out Gender-Assigned Roles

"A woman's work is never done" is one of the phrases that haunts us, like a poltergeist disturbing the rational thought of normally sane men

- With our help, my daughter must pick up her toys at the end of the day (this happens about 50 percent of the time). Specifically, she puts her shoes in the closet, dirty clothes in the hamper, and puts all her books back on the shelf.
- Our bedroom is always a mess. For some reason, it's our last priority. But we have agreed to loosely make the bed every day, and we have a dresser that we call our "relationship mantle," where we put pictures, cards, sea shells from vacations, and special treasures from our children. We are not allowed to put anything else on top of this dresser. It's the one clean space in the room that doesn't have mail, folded clothes, or books piled high. And it feels great.

We cannot live up to our own standards all the time. This is our realistic ideal—and the compromise within our two comfort zones. The point of coming to an agreement with your partner and writing it down helps you understand each other's expectations and needs—and ensures that you are on the same team. It's good to know—especially when the house is a disaster—that your partner sees a vision of cleanliness, like a mirage in the desert, that's in harmony with yours.

and women. It's the same mode of thinking that reinforces other negative and false stereotypes. And it deserves the same fate as other phrases, such as "sports are for men"—which was debunked thanks to Title IX (which increased girls' participation in high school sports by ten times), a Women's World Cup Soccer Championship, and the Women's National Basketball Association, to name just a few. Or "Women aren't meant to run companies"—which you might want to mention to Meg Whitman, CEO of eBay, or Carly Fiorina, CEO of Hewlett Packard. And there's always "Leave politics to the men," although don't mention that to Condoleeza Rice, Hilary Clinton, or

Nancy Pelosi. A mere 30 years ago, many people truly didn't believe women belonged in college and professional sports, executive management, or politics. Women belonged in the kitchen, doing—you guessed it—women's work. Slowly but triumphantly, the idea of women's work is beginning to take on a new meaning.

Women concede that once they have children, they often fall back into traditional roles and take on responsibilities that they are "supposed" to. The problems with traditional gender-assigned tasks is that they are based on a mostly outdated model that assumes that women must do just about everything for the home and children, and men must fulfill their role as providers. And women, supported by the Mother Martyr and her endless appetite for all drudge tasks, are sucked into thinking that it's their duty—and that they're better at taking care of the home than men. Even today, with the vast majority of mothers working, women are still largely responsible for grocery shopping, cooking, dishwashing, housecleaning, and laundry. These are the tasks that make up the bulk of the day-to-day housework, and they pile up as quickly as you can say, "Hire a housecleaner." Traditional men's tasks, on the other hand, are often done weekly or monthly, such as yard work, home repair, and, of course, "the garbage," the Mustang GT of men's chores. In fact, my husband feels emasculated if I take out the garbage myself. "Why did you do that?" he demands, his virility clearly having masked the stench of garbage in the house for the past day.

As Scott Coltrane writes, "Recent research confirms that family work is sharply divided by gender, with women spending much more time on these tasks than men and typically taking responsibility for monitoring and supervising the work, even when they pay for domestic services or delegate tasks to others." Surprisingly, he adds, "Although the vast majority of both men and women agree that family labor should be shared, few men assume equal responsibility for household tasks. On average, women perform two to three times as much housework as men, and the vast majority . . . rate these arrangements as fair."

Top 10 Gender-Associated Tasks

Which of these tasks do you or your partner take on automatically—whether or not it has been discussed or negotiated—or out of a sense of guilt? Which tasks are most time-consuming, and which are daily or occasional?

1. Men take out the garbage.
2. Women cook.
3. Men take care of the cars.
4. Women manage the laundry.
5. Men handle loan documents.
6. Women grocery shop.
7. Men manage recycling.
8. Women mop the floors.
9. Men organize the garage.
10. Women clean the bathroom.

If you find that you have broken out of some of these traditional molds—your husband cooks, you handle the finances and oil changes—then you are already on the road to discovering what works in your relationship. You may find yourself comfortable with many of these items—and feel that you're okay with them.

Take time to look at the task you've been pushed into: Margaret, mother of two, realized that on weekends she was always inside doing routine indoor housecleaning, and her husband was always outside in the fresh air doing special projects. She wanted to be gardening or raking or building, but felt that it was her first duty to clean the inside of the house, until she really looked at her assumptions and learned that her husband was happy to switch with her—or better yet, to work side-by-side, outdoors, with their kids playing or helping. Lucy tells me that painting her two daughters' bedroom, installing shelves, and refinishing their furniture was rewarding and gave her a sense of her own physical ability. Just as we can feel empowered, men also enjoy crossing the gender line in the sand. In many couples I spoke with, the husband was the primary cook or the neatnik. Don't let your gender dictate the job description.

Step Three: Negotiate Areas of Expertise

Martha is a mother of one who works part-time as a researcher in the social sciences and equally shares most of the household responsibilities with her husband Kevin, a financial manager, based on who does what best. "For years we tried to keep track of each chore and split it evenly, so that neither person would do too much or too little. That was horribly stressful and seemed to pit us against each other and left us feeling unappreciated. Now we each do what we enjoy—or at least don't hate to do—and are good at. I've accepted the fact that Kevin will never, ever clean a bathroom. But he does the majority of vacuuming and much the dishes. He does all of the finances (something I would hate to do), but I do almost all of our social planning and gift-giving."

Choosing the tasks that you enjoy doing is good couple management, but be careful that you don't just choose what you think you're good at—for most women believe they're better at most household tasks. Remember, it's not an innate skill, but rather lifelong training that has made some of us consummate toilet scrubbers, so your partner, too, can acquire this skill and many others.

Often, such as in Martha and Kevin's case, negotiating to your strengths works well. But it can also create an unfair division of labor, as Rhona Mahony points out in *Kidding Ourselves*. When children arrive, time becomes a limited resource. We tend to fall into roles of doing what we do best or specialize in, thus helping us save time, which is called gains of specialization. For example, since I do such a fine job of mopping the floor—beginning with my childhood training based on gender—I mop the floor all the time. Mahony points out though, that "in many families the pressure to specialize pushes the woman toward a more traditional sexual division of labor . . ." where

Designing Your Ideal Routine

Discuss your nightly routine. You are both working—maybe one of you is taking care of the children; the other is working outside the home. Or maybe you are both working outside the home. At the end of the day you are tired. The kids are finally in bed or at least sequestered in their rooms, and the house needs a quickie cleanup, dishes and all.

- What usually happens at this time?
- What would you like to happen?
- What was the habit for your family growing up?
- How can you come to an agreement about your responsibility during this time that works for your family now?

Equal Partners Story

Roma and Peter consider that "equal parenting" time begins once they are to-gether at the end of the day. If one has been home with the kids all day and one working outside the home, they have both been working. Peter and Roma both work a flex-time workweek, and they appreciate how each role—the working parent and the stay-at-home parent—is taxing in its own way. Roma says, "Once we're home, Peter never assumes that I will feed the kids or do the dishes, and vice versa. We communicate very clearly. Often, the person who is burned out on parenting all day is desperate to make dinner and clean the kitchen, and the person who worked in front of a computer is anxious to connect with the children and help with homework and the bedtime routine. Sometimes, though, it's a grind and we're both exhausted. It's an incredible re-lief to have an active partner during this time—and not somebody who kicks back and puts feet up on the couch or emotionally checks out. We can finish all the essential cleaning quickly and then spend time together."

the woman ends up doing more and more unpaid labor. In other words, because we have so much to do and so little time, we end up associating tasks with the person who is most efficient. Although it's tempting to take advantage of the gains of specialization—and it can be beneficial in many ways—make sure you're not entrapping your-self and keeping your husband from learning how to be efficient on his own.

Rachel, mother of a toddler, has worked out a good balance with her partner. "I am really good at keeping numerous things afloat in my mental schedule, so I am usually the one to plan our social life. I hate doing dishes, and my husband abhors folding and sorting laundry, so we have compromised here. We both like to cook, so it's not a problem for either of us to prepare meals. I do most errands and phone calls. I think our compromising and duty-sharing is essential for our relationship, and it's a great model for our daughter: There are so many responsibilities in life, and you have to be able to support your loved ones and allow them to support you."

Step Four: Break Down How You Spend Your Time

Time is one of the most limited resources as a parent. There is never enough of it to go around. My husband is often fighting the clock, while I've taken the opposite approach and stopped wearing a watch the day I had my first baby. Whatever your relation to time, almost all of the couples I've spoken with feel that, at any given time, they are devoting inadequate attention to either children, work, or their relationship. We all seem to be overwhelmed with the endless, thankless tasks involved in just maintaining a home, yet we're deeply committed to the rewarding effort of creating a loving and rich environment. The hours in the day are simply not there, it seems.

Understanding how each of you spend time will help you find creative ways to fulfill the family's needs—and make sure you're getting some of your own personal needs met. If you look at the hours you spend working, commuting, with children, and driving, it's revealing to see the breakdown. You might feel relieved: "Oh, this is why I'm not getting enough work done or my kids miss me so much." When he was working full-time, my husband realized that during certain heavy workweeks he was only seeing the children 30 minutes a day before bedtime, while I was seeing them 7 hours—and we were both working, albeit he a longer day with a commute. It might suddenly shed light on why you're just not able to get done

Evaluate Your Time: Not Enough Hours in the Day

It's important that both you and your partner do this and are honest with yourself about how you're spending your time. Some common categories of tasks are below. Also, we know that multitasking is the stuff of life, so you might have two columns with the same hours. Try to pick the main task (for example, during child care you're doing housework, during work hours you're doing finances).

Task	Daily Hours	Weekly Hours
Work		
Commute		
Driving		
Child care		
Food prep		
Housework		
Personal		
Other		
TOTAL		

It's important to examine your time evaluations together and see where they're inequitable. Obviously, if someone is working 20 hours a week and someone else is working 45, the part-time worker will pick up more child care and housework. It's important to note, though, when there are imbalances and if they make sense. For example, does one spouse spend 12 hours a week working out, and the other person is not able to make it to the gym? Does one person do all meal preparation even though both are working comparable hours outside of the home? What are you giving up that you shouldn't give up, such as sleep? Look at the numbers, discuss if you're comfortable with them, and see how you can begin to make changes.

what you want to get done—or, as June said, "My husband is spending 20 hours a week on playing computer games. Hello?! Twenty hours a week! I'd like to have just 3 hours a week for myself."

Instead of focusing on the definitions of fairness in housework, strive to reestablish your commitment to your partnership. Many women talked about how their husbands were better at asking for personal time for working out or hobbies and realized it was a source of resentment. "When I have a spare few minutes, say during naptime," Teri explained, "I run around picking things up, throwing laundry in the washer, and only rarely will I put my feet up. Kevin is much better at stopping doing chores to run out and meet a friend or play his guitar for a half hour. I admire this, but it also irritates me that I cannot let go of my constant sense of responsibility for the family."

Breaking down the hours gives you a snapshot of your life together and helps you prioritize. Are you working too much—and do you have any control over this? How can you take 5 hours a week to exercise? Can you have one night a week for a career development course? How can you spend more time together as a family in some fun activity, not just routine? Does the time you spend reflect your values and goals? Asking yourself these questions can inform your life in miraculous new ways.

Step Five: Get Children to Contribute

Babies are adorable, but they aren't much help around the house. So, hallelujah when you can begin to incorporate your children into the household routines. I remember my mother teaching me how to clean the bathroom, under the rim, around the bolts on the floor—a lesson that my brother managed to miss because of gender. Things have changed, though, and you can teach both boys and girls the skills and art of maintaining a house. (Remember to teach your daughters how to change the oil on the car as well as teaching sons how to clean the toilet.) Not only is it important to be part of the family community, but a child's home is a part of their emotional development. Clare Cooper Marcus writes, "A child constructing a den or clubhouse under the hedge is doing far more than merely manipulating dirt and branches. He or she is having a powerful experience of creativity, of learning about self via molding the physical environment. In adolescence, posters fixed to the bedroom wall, photos displayed, clothes left in disarray—all may make a statement to parents: This is who I am! I am my own person, even if I'm not quite sure yet who that is."

From an early age, children are able to contribute, beginning with clearing their plate, setting the table, and picking up toys and their own messes. As they get older, it's important to instill a sense of pride in their work and that they are part of a living community. I call it family teamwork. The more your children are self-reliant, independent, and conscious of their use of the house, the happier the family, and the happier adults they will become. By teaching them responsibility for their environment and the family community, you are doing them a great service. Here are some suggestions to help incorporate your kids into your household routine.

※ Make a chart, with the help of your children, that spells out exactly what each child's responsibility is—with gold stars or stickers signifying achievement. Even if your children cannot yet read, the process of doing this together will give it a level of seriousness and accountability that feels good to both parents and children.

※ Let your children know they are active contributors of managing the household. Teach them to notice what needs doing and add to your family goals list. Assign them the task of managing the grocery list and adding needed items instead of complaining about having no food in the house. (Better yet: Make a computer-generated list with your standard items, and organize it so that it corresponds with aisles in the grocery store!)

✳ Spend time teaching your children how to do one task: load the dishwasher correctly; fold clothes; fill out forms; call for a dentist appointment for themselves. Be intentional about the task, not simply correcting them once they've done it wrong, but committing to teaching them properly, with patience and diligence.

✳ Our natural and family resources are precious commodities. Our family resources might be about time together or material goods: We don't eat on the couch, because we want to take care of our things. It's just as critical to teach our children to respect natural resources by turning out lights, not running water while brushing teeth, not wasting food, and not abusing nature and property. We must teach our children to recycle waste products and explain how our actions impact the environment.

✳ Allowance, if given when chores are completed in a timely manner, can promote financial responsibility and money management, teach the value of money, and offer an incentive to kids that can be pulled back if they're not upholding their end of the chore bargain.

Final Step: Assign Housework and Family Culture Goals—Together

I remember when our second child was just a baby, I met my husband in the driveway as he pulled in after work with, "Guess what? I went to the drycleaners today." "Life is good," he responded with a big smile. We enjoyed a quiet moment of triumph before it dawned on us how sorry our life really was: getting to the drycleaner was a family cause for celebration. (Never mind that it was a full 3 weeks after I promised to go after hearing him mention that he was out of clean work shirts.) Where had our priority-making ability gone?

The Family Standard of Cleanliness gives us a framework for creating daily priorities and making choices about family needs. It makes perfect sense to go to the park on the first gorgeous day of spring instead of reorganizing the basement. Other times, it's not so clear what the family priorities should be: You might want to shop, and he might want to do yard work. He might want to go to the ball game with the kids, and you might feel that they need to do homework and chores. Communicating at the micro level about household priorities clears the way for guilt-free and bicker-free time together. As Cynthia, a nurse and mother of one explains, "I never thought I'd be able to do it, but when the choice is to wash the kitchen floor or to go out together for a walk on the weekends, I usually choose the latter and am glad. Also, we keep a list of one-time household projects that need to be done—not ongoing cleaning—prominently posted in the kitchen. We both consult it when we have time on the weekends. This way, neither of us has to nag the other to do something. We can each choose what we want from the list, and this way most things do get done."

For long-term goals and special projects, I have created the mother of all lists (or perhaps I should say the father of all lists). If crossing items off of to-do lists makes you giddy, this list will not disappoint. Looking at the categories of needs, it's easy to see if you have balance in your family—do you have too many home improvement projects and not enough socializing? Are you spending all your money on vacations, yet your car is breaking down? Keeping the list current, having both partners actively involved in the maintenance of the list by crossing things off and adding new items helps you feel a sense of accomplishment, responsibility, and progress. Here are the suggested categories.

House Goals include home improvement/maintenance, purchases, cleaning, and organization.

Family Goals include vacation, nutrition, health, projects, car maintenance, behavioral standards, and purchases.

Community Goals include socializing, volunteering, party planning, friendships, activism, and more.

Ultimately, Family Culture Goals help you prioritize what's most important in your life—and to let go of the other stuff. We all have things that need to be done all the time. Parenting and running a household is a never-ending job. Stopping to appreciate your family and the strides you've made—and prioritizing what's truly important—is just as important as the accomplishment itself.

To create your goals for this chapter, start with House Goals, Family Goals, and Community Goals as the main categories—and of course add any others or change them to fit your family. Include the "owner" of the task, the task itself, and the month you intend to accomplish the item. It's fun to update and cross items off the list. You'll feel a great sense of completion and progress. Here is an example of what the list might look like.

Family Culture Goals

Who	Task	When
House Goals		
John	Trim trees	Sept
Rachel	Set up crib for baby	Oct
Rachel	Paint dollhouse for Christmas	Oct–Nov
John	Fire alarm check and maintenance	Oct
Rachel/John	Clean and organize basement	Jan

Who	Task	When
Family Goals		
Rachel/John	Plan Spring vacation	Sept
Rachel	Emergency preparation kit	Oct
All	Trip to great-grandparents	Sept
Rachel	Update photo albums	Nov–Dec
Rachel/John	Research electric/gas hybrid cars	Nov–Dec
All	Eat more fruit for dessert, less sugar!	Ongoing

NEGOTIATION POINTS

This chart provides a starting point to define and assign your family's tasks. It's a laundry list, so to speak, of the functions involved in running our households, divided up into the following categories:

Everyday Tasks, which happen daily, such as meal preparation

Ongoing Tasks, which happen regularly, but not daily, such as cleaning a bathroom or mowing the lawn

Special Tasks, which are more infrequent or tied to a special event, such as cleaning the gutters or preparing for holiday celebrations.

There may be several ways for you to accomplish these tasks. Obviously, you and your partner and your children are the primary doers, but some families may also hire outside help. From preparing food to laundry to cleaning, there are many services now offered that are not cost-prohibitive and are a boon to busy working parents. Don't hesitate to pick up the prepared roast chicken and frozen peas at the grocery store, if it frees up time to spend with your children and relieves some pressure on your relationship with your spouse. Having a twice-monthly housecleaner has saved many marriages.

Keep in mind that the most time-consuming tasks, in order, are meal preparation and cooking, housecleaning, shopping for groceries and household goods, washing dishes, meal cleanup, and laundry. Clearly, feeding the family is the biggie. Also, while you are assigning the tasks, consider:

* Time availability
* Your Family Standard of Cleanliness and Family Culture priorities
* Who enjoys the task or is better suited for it
* Whether you need external resources to help you with this task and who will manage these resources
* Adding Special Tasks to your Family Culture Goals (above), when appropriate

Task	Everyday	Ongoing	Special
Feeding Our Family			
Meal planning			
Breakfast			
Lunch			
Dinner			
Shopping list			
Grocery shopping			
School lunches			
Meal preparation			
Dishes and cleanup			
Unloading dishwasher			
Overall kitchen cleanup (mopping floors, etc.)			
The Work of the House			
House clutter pickup			
Mail sorting			
Garbage			

Task	Everyday	Ongoing	Special
Recycling			
Dusting			
Floors: vacuuming, sweeping			
Bathroom cleaning			
Organization (closets, drawers, cabinets)			
Garage			
Cleaning drawers			
Managing Laundry			
Bringing into washroom			
Separating, loading, washing			
Folding			
Putting Away			
Changing Sheets			
Organizing linen closets			
Home Repair			
Fixing and repairing			
Calling service people			
Insurance claims			
Outdoor Maintenance			
Washing windows			
Sweeping			
Lawn			
Raking			
Weeding			
Gardening			
Winter/Summer maintenance			
Trips to dump or recycling center			

Task	Everyday	Ongoing	Special
Extreme weather preparation			
Family Sustenance			
Weekend activity planning			
Social calendar			
Planning date nights			
Arranging for babysitter			
Planning vacations			
Packing for trips			
Community involvement			
Environmental education			
Social Graces			
Gift-giving			
Thank-you notes			
Returning phone calls			
Calling relatives			
Holiday Planning			
Keeping the Car Running			
Keeping car clean			
Regular oil changes			
Car servicing/parts			
Children's Involvement			
Creation of chore lists			
Adding items to shopping lists			
Teaching how to do household tasks			
Method of accountability			

A Husband's Viewpoint

The Day-to-Day Drudgery

When I was working full-time, we had a housecleaner come in once a week, and I thought that took care of cleaning our house. When I arrived home from work, things were always pretty much picked up. Karen had put away most toys, done the dinner prep dishes (but not always!), and if occasionally things were wild and messy—those times usually coincided with hectic work schedules for both of us. It was easy to ignore it, though, since I just left for work in the morning. I knew someone would take care of it while I was at work. And it usually wasn't me.

Now that I'm home more, I'm in a state of shock. Yesterday, I think I cleaned the floor under the highchair 14 times (that's sweeping and mopping). And the kitchen was still messy at the end of the day. The little things the kids leave everywhere, like hair clips and blocks and Matchbox cars, drive me crazy. I cannot believe how they can demolish the house in 20 short minutes. It's more frustrating than I expected. It's even more frustrating because I know Karen thinks I should do a better job at it. I feel her critical eye, which makes me feel resentful and defensive and like not doing a thing. But I persist and am getting better at everything, like grocery shopping and getting the kids ready for school in the morning. It takes practice, I tell myself, and I'm still a rookie.

INTENTION: COMMIT TO CONTRIBUTING EQUALLY TO MANAGING THE HOME

"Honey, you take care of it. Just have the cleaner come more often" isn't the support I was looking for when I told Gill I was frustrated with our messy home. Both men and women throw this so-called solution out when being asked to contribute more. In other words, he was saying that his time was too valuable to help around the house. Hire someone at a lower wage to take care of it—but we know that this solution is neither affordable nor 100 percent effective. There is no avoiding the minutiae that must be done every single day. And it is a parent who must take responsibility for it.

Taking Care of Home and Hearth Intention Statement:

We commit to being equally responsible for finding solutions that support a healthy, loving family environment.

_____   _____
Signed   Signed

Afterword

hen I started researching and writing this book, Gill and I were still figuring out how we wanted to parent our kids, what was best for our family, and how to make the mechanics of equal parenting work. I would often start interviews with full disclosure: "I am *not* a great example of equal parenting, by the way." I wanted people to know that I understood how difficult it was to formally choose to be equal parents—and that Gill and I were a well-meaning, disheveled work in progress.

In the beginning, my quest for equal parenting was met with heavy resistance from Gill that brought lots of complaining and unhappiness from me. At one point, Gill actually asked me: "Weren't you raised knowing you would one day give up everything for your children and support your husband?" Of course, he denies he ever said this (just as I reserve the right to deny things I have said in the heat of negotiating our family roles). In the transition of going from an un-encumbered, selfish couple to a couple with children, Gill was afraid of losing his identity, of losing career momentum, of losing personal freedom. I was afraid of the same things—and with good reason. I felt as if they had all, in fact, happened to me in varying degrees in the years following the births of our children. I feared being stuck at home, losing my identity, having my brain turn to mush, losing financial independence and my status in the world, and, on top of that, I felt guilty for not wanting to be with my children every minute of every day—guilty for wanting a life alongside my family life.

But as Gill and I threw ourselves into our roles as parents, we realized that having children was not about loss. It was about gain: gaining a new world perspective; new dimensions to our life; and the feelings of love for our children that go beyond word. We realized that our life, right now, is about making our family and marriage strong and loving our children and each other as much as possible. This is a difficult task in the best of circumstances, but becomes close to impossible when one spouse works extremely long hours outside the home. When I started this book, Gill was working full-time and was out of the house about 65 to 70 hours a week. He would often go days without seeing the children during his workweek, and I would feel alone and overburdened as I managed working from home, caring for the children, and everything else. This was unacceptable to both of us: Gill missed the children and they missed him; I missed my husband and wasn't happy being a single parent during the week.

More than anything I said or did, it was simply the love of our children that influenced us to make a dramatic shift in our family. We began to evaluate our life in the San Francisco Bay Area. We lived in a community where family and friends surrounded us, but we were frustrated by the fast pace and high cost of living. We committed our intention—equal parenting—to paper, crossing our fingers that we would find a way to live what was in our hearts.

Guess what? It worked. Because of our conscious intention to find a way to make equal parenting a priority, we made decisions that have led us to a new chapter in our lives. As I finish this book, I am working a full-time position in a different town in a different state, where the pace of life is much slower. Although no longer working at home, my commute is only 5 minutes—and after working at home for 5 years, I'm enjoying getting out of the house. Gill is thriving in his role as primary parent, and is still able to work 25 or so hours a week from home. We're happy in our role reversals—and glad to have a more balanced home and work life.

I confess there have been moments of gleeful observation—for both of us: I have enjoyed watching him fully grasp the lack of personal freedom the primary parent has. At the same time, Gill is thrilled to be with the children and does not miss the demands of his former high-stress job. Sometimes I'm shocked at how completely our roles have switched. When I come home from work, I want to grab a beer and sit on the couch, and it's hard for me not to ask, "What's for dinner? Don't we have any food in the house?" The other day I came home and he needed to show and tell me of all he had done: the food he had bought, the clothes he had folded, the phone calls he made; and I, with full understanding, gave him appreciation and kudos for his superior parenting and grocery shopping skills.

The other day Gill asked me, in all seriousness, "Why don't we have any casserole recipes? They're such good leftovers!" He left the room irritated that I'd never mastered the casserole—and I burst out laughing. "I've made it," I thought. "We did it."

Acknowledgments

I am in gratitude to the women and men I interviewed for the book. Your candidness and desire to explore the issue of equal parenting was inspiring. I have much respect and appreciation for the scholars whose work I referenced: Scott Coltrane at University of California, Irvine, Rosalind Barnett and Karen Gareis at Brandeis University, Shelley A. Haddock and Toni S. Zimmerman at Colorado State University, Stephanie Coontz at Evergreen State College, Patricia Voydanoff at the University of Dayton, Rhona Rapoport at the Institute of Family and Environmental Research, Joan Williams at American University, Rhona Mahony at Stanford and many others doing important work exploring work and family dynamics. This expanding field of study gives me great hope. I also appreciate the work of Ellen Galinsky, *Ms. Magazine*, *Working Mother* magazine, Ann Crittenden, Harriet Lerner, Natalie Angier, Sue Schellenberger, and many others who have influenced me in all sorts of ways.

My incredible community of support gives me equal parts feedback, pep talks, and camaraderie. I am grateful for those who shared their personal stories, read the book at various stages, or provided much-needed empathy when I hadn't slept for 6 months: Sheila, Diane, Emily, Peggy, Jackie, Matthew, Seana, Maurice, Mary Jane, Emily, Micheline, and Arthur. Loving and rooting for me are my parents Mike and Jill, Alan and Amy, and the Newtons. I appreciate the diligence and personal interest of my agent, John Silbersack, father of three; my editor, Lou Cinquino, father of two; and editorial mavens Jill Stern and Amy Morgan.

Finally, my family. I am graced with two precious children who break my heart wide open every single day and a lovely, devoted partner, my husband, Gill. My children challenge me to be the best person I can be: It's an honor, privilege, and extraordinary gift to be their mother. And to my husband, a man who will settle for nothing less than an exceptional marriage and is willing to do what it takes to achieve this, I thank you for raising the bar.

CHAPTER 1

p. 4   [. . . still suffering . . .] Barnett, Rosalind and Caryl Rivers. *She Works/He Works: How Two-Income Families are Happier, Healthier, and Better Off.* San Francisco: HarperSanFrancisco, 1996.

p. 8   [. . . still 'women's work' . . .] Jones, Jacqueline. American Work: Four Centuries of Black and White Labor New York: W.W. Norton & Company, 1998.

p. 11   [. . . housework with their fathers . . .] Coltrane, Scott and Michele Adams. University of California, Riverside, 2003. Coltrane and Adams examined data from the Child Development Supplement of the Panel Study of Income Dynamics.

p. 14   [. . . resented the monotony . . .] Yalom, Marilyn. *A History of the Wife.* New York: HarperCollins, 2001, p. 369.

p. 16   [. . . finding new ways to parent . . .] Barnett, Rosalind and Caryl Rivers (1996) op. cit., p. 400.

p. 17   [. . . responsibility for inequality . . .] Taylor, Maurice and Seana McGee. *The New Couple: Why the Old Rules Don't Work and What Does.* San Francisco: Harper SanFrancisco, 2000.

p. 17   [. . . successful dual-earner marriages . . .] Haddock, Shelley A., Toni Schindler Zimmerman, Scott J. Ziemba, and Lisa R. Current. "Ten Adaptive Strategies for Family and Work Balance: Advice from Successful Families." *Journal of Marital and Family Therapy* 27, no. 4 (October 2001).

CHAPTER 2

p. 29   [. . . naturally inclined to motherhood . . .] Angier, Natalie. *Woman: An Intimate Geography*. Boston: Houghton Mifflin, 1999.

p. 32   [. . . children the raison d'être . . .] Hayt, Elizabeth. Admitting to Mixed Feelings about Motherhood. *The New York Times*, 12 May 2002.

p. 33   [. . . keeps women silent . . .] Maushart, Susan. *The Mask of Motherhood: How Becoming a Mother Changes Everything and Why We Pretend It Doesn't*. New York: New Press, 1999.

p. 36   [. . . women of the '70s . . .] Priest, Ruth. The Failure of Feminism. *San Jose Mercury News*, 25 March 2002.

p. 40   [. . . people still believe . . .] Hart and Teeter/NBC/Wall Street Journal Poll. The Family: People's Chief Concerns, June 1999.

p. 40   [. . . 83 percent of us believe . . .] Pew Research Center for the People and Press. 1999 Millennial Survey.

p. 40   [. . . two-thirds of parents say . . .] Ibid.

p. 42   [. . . cultivate guilt . . .] Lerner, Harriet. *The Mother Dance: How Children Change Your Life*. New York: HarperCollins, 1998.

p. 43   [. . . splintered and disenfranchised . . .] Berry, Cecelie S. "Home Is Where the Revolution Is." *Salon* online magazine, 29 September 1999.

p. 44   [. . . supportive women . . .] Diamant, Anita. *The Red Tent*. New York: St. Martin's Press, 1997. This bestselling book is a fictionalized account of biblical stories. It gives a vivid, wonderful picture of a supportive environment of women who create a sanctuary in their red tent, where they celebrate menstruation, birth, death, and illness (if you can get past the polygamy!).

p. 49   [. . . gatekeeping . . .] Braun-Levine, Susan. *Father Courage: What Happens When Men Put Family First*. New York: Harcourt, 2000.

p. 49   [. . . mother management . . .] Orenstein, Peggy. *Flux: Women on Sex, Work, Love, Kids & Life in a Half-Changed World*. New York: Doubleday, 2000.

p. 50   [. . . protect the family . . .] Schwartz, Pepper. *Peer Marriage: How Love Between Equals Really Works*. New York: Free Press, 1994.

p. 55   [. . . women play sports . . .] Nelson, Mariah Burton. And Now They Tell Us Women Don't Really Like Sports? *Ms. Magazine*, Winter 2002.

CHAPTER 3

p. 66   [. . . greatest challenge to a couple . . .] Hanson, Rick, Jan Hanson, and Ricki Pollycove. *Mother Nurture: A Mother's Guide to Health in Body, Mind, and Intimate Relationships*. New York: Penguin USA, 2002.

p. 81   [. . . relationship book . . .] Taylor, Maurice and Seana McGee. *The New Couple: Why the Old Rules Don't Work and What Does.* San Francisco: Harper San-Francisco, 2000.

CHAPTER 4

p. 109   [. . . balance in their lives . . .] Wolf, Naomi. *Misconceptions: Truth, Lies, and the Unexpected on the Journey to Motherhood* New York: Doubleday, 2001.

p. 110   [. . . wife as the high wage earner . . .] Tyre, Peg and Daniel McGinn. She Works, He Doesn't. *Newsweek*, 12 May 2003. Statistics gathered from Bureau of Labor Statistics data and analyzed by University of Maryland demographer Suzanne Bianchi.

p. 110   [. . . rhetoric of choice . . .] Crittenden, Ann. *The Price of Motherhood: Why the Most Important Job is the Least Valued.* New York: Metropolitan Books, 2001.

p. 113   [. . . career ambition . . .] Hrdy, Sarah Blaffer. Scientist at Work: Sarah Blaffer Hrdy; Primate Expert Explores Motherhood's Brutal Side. Interview by Natalie Angier. *New York Times*, 8 February 2000.

p. 114   [. . . requesting part-time work . . .] Rhona Mahony . *Kidding Ourselves: Breadwinning, Babies, and Bargaining.* New York: Basic Books, 1995.

p. 115   [. . . giving up work . . .] Warner, Judith. Why We Work. *Working Mother*, September 2001.

p. 115   [. . . Census Bureau publication . . .] Lewin, Tamar. Now a Majority: Families with 2 Parents Who Work. *New York Times*, 24 October 2000.

p. 115   [. . . dual-income families . . .] Ibid.

p. 116   [. . . married women like to work . . .] Yalom, Marilyn. *A History of the Wife.* New York: HarperCollins, 2001.

p. 116   [. . . better emotional health . . .] Barnett, Rosalind and Caryl Rivers. *She Works/He Works: How Two-Income Families are Happier, Healthier, and Better Off.* San Francisco: HarperSanFrancisco, 1996, p. 28.

p. 118   [. . . excellent role models . . .] Orenstein, Peggy. *Flux: Women on Sex, Work, Love, Kids & Life in a Half-Changed World.* New York: Doubleday, 2000.

p. 119   [. . . mothers have worked . . .] Hrdy, Sarah Blaffer. Interview by Susan Caba. *Salon* online magazine, 9 December 1999.

p. 120   [. . . domestic chores . . .] Lake, Dianne. Make the Dough, Do the Laundry: Life as a Breadwinner Mom. *Salon* online magazine, 5 October 1999.

p. 121   [. . . choosing part-time employment . . .] Wenger, Jeffrey. The Continuing Problems with Part-Time Jobs. Economic Policy Institute Issue Brief #155, 24 April 2001.

p. 121   [. . . reduce their work hours . . .] Barnett, Rosalind. When a Part-time Job Equals Full-Time Work. Interview by Marilyn Gardner. *Christian Science Monitor*, 19 February 2003.

p. 124   [. . . women continue to work . . .] Warner, Judith (September 2001) op. cit.

p. 124   [. . . 100 women physicians . . .] Barnett, Rosalind (2003) op. cit.

p. 124   [. . . median income . . .] U.S. Census Bureau. March 1997 Current Population Survey.

p. 130   [. . . new mathematics . . .] Clarkberg, Marin. "The Time Squeeze in American Families" in Balancing Acts: Easing the Burdens and Improving the Options for Working Families. Economic Policy Institute, April 2000.

p. 130   [. . . current gender system . . .] Williams, Joan. *Unbending Gender: Why Family and Work Conflict and What to Do About It.* New York: Oxford University Press, 2000.

p. 133   [. . . between a woman and a meal . . .] Angier, Natalie. *Woman: An Intimate Geography.* Boston: Houghton Mifflin, 1999.

p. 133   [. . . predominant myths of the day . . .] Lerner, Harriet. *The Mother Dance: How Children Change Your Life.* New York: HarperCollins, 1998.

p. 136   [. . . Second Women's Movement . . .] Corrigan, Maureen. The Trials of Juggling a Baby and a Briefcase. *The New York Times*, 8 May 2002.

CHAPTER 5

p. 151   [. . . show them how . . .] Martin, William C. *The Parent's Tao Te Ching: Ancient Advice for Modern Parents: A New Interpretation.* New York: Marlowe & Company, 1999.

p. 157   [. . . day-to-day management . . .] Maushart, Susan. *The Mask of Motherhood: How Becoming a Mother Changes Everything and Why We Pretend It Doesn't.* New York: New Press, 1999.

p. 158   [. . . realities facing parents . . .] Phillips, Deborah and Gina Adams. Childcare and Our Youngest Children. *The Future of Children* 11, no. 1 (Spring/Summer 2001).

p. 159   [. . . day care providers . . .] Greenspan, Stanley, with Jacqueline Salmon. *The Four-Thirds Solution: Solving the Childcare Crisis in America Today.* New York: Perseus, 2001.

p. 161   [. . . blaming mom . . .] Barnett, Rosalind C., and Rivers, Caryl. *She Works/He Works: How Two-Income Families are Happier, Healthier, and Better Off.* San Francisco: HarperSanFrancisco, 1996.

p. 163   [. . . Fatherly devotion . . .] Angier, Natalie. *Woman: An Intimate Geography.* Boston: Houghton Mifflin, 1999.

p. 172   [. . . family happiness . . .] Haddock, Shelley A., Zimmerman, Toni Schindler, Ziemba, Scott J., and Current, Lisa R. Ten Adaptive Strategies for Family and Work Balance: Advice from Successful Families. *Journal of Marital and Family Therapy* 27, no. 4 (October 2001).

p. 176   [. . . parents today worry more . . .] Anderegg, David. *Worried All the Time: Overparenting in an Age of Anxiety and How to Stop It*. New York: Free Press, 2003.

p. 177   [. . . emotional intelligence . . .] Levant, Ronald F., M.D. with Kopecky, Gina. *Masculinity Reconstructed: Changing the Rules of Manhood at Work, in Relationships, and in Family Life*. New York: Dutton, 1995.

CHAPTER 6

p. 189   [. . . Keeping house . . .] Mendelson, Cheryl. *Home Comforts : The Art and Science of Keeping House*. New York: Scribner, 1999.

p. 191   [. . . home fulfills many needs . . .] Marcus, Clare Cooper. *House As a Mirror of Self*. Berkeley, California: Conari Press, 1995.

p. 199   [. . . roles were clear-cut . . .] Yalom, Marilyn. *A History of the Wife*. New York: HarperCollins, 2001.

p. 203   [. . . balance of power . . .] Coltrane, Scott. *Family Man: Fatherhood, Housework, and Gender Equity*. New York: Oxford University Press, 1997.

p. 212   [. . . divided by gender . . .] Coltrane, Scott. Research on Household Labor: Modeling and Measuring the Social Embeddedness of Routine Family Work. *Journal of Marriage and the Family* 62, 2000.

p. 215   [. . . pressure to specialize . . .] Mahony, Rhona. *Kidding Ourselves: Breadwinning, Babies, and Bargaining*. New York: Basic Books, 1995.

p. 220   [. . . learning about self . . .] Marcus, Clare Cooper (1995) op. cit.

Bibliography

Angier, Natalie. Woman: *An Intimate Geography*. Boston: Houghton Mifflin, 1999.

Barnett, Rosalind C. and Caryl Rivers. *She Works/He Works: How Two-Income Families are Happier, Healthier, and Better Off*. San Francisco: HarperSanFrancisco, 1996.

Blakely, Mary Kay. *American Mom: Motherhood, Politics, and Humble Pie*. North Carolina: Algonquin Books of Chapel Hill, 1994.

Crittenden, Ann. *The Price of Motherhood: Why the Most Important Job in the World Is the Least Valued*. New York: Metropolitan Books, 2001.

Ehrenreich, Barbara, and Arlie Russell Hochschild. *Global Woman: Nannies, Maids, and Sex Workers in the New Economy*. New York: Metropolitan Books, Henry Holt and Company, 2002.

Greenspan, Stanley with Jacqueline Salmon. *The Four-Thirds Solution: Solving the Child-care Crisis in America*. New York: Perseus, 2001.

Hanson, Rick, Jan Hanson, and Ricki Pollycove. *Mother Nurture: A Mother's Guide to Health in Body, Mind, and Intimate Relationships*. New York: Penguin USA, 2002.

Hochschild, Arlie with Anne Machung. *The Second Shift: Working Parents and the Revolution at Home*. New York: Viking Penguin, 1989.

Hrdy, Sarah Blaffer. *Mother Nature: A History of Mothers, Infants, and Natural Selection*. New York: Pantheon, 1999.

Lerner, Harriet. *The Mother Dance: How Children Change Your Life*. New York: Harper-Collins, 1998.

Mahony, Rhona. *Kidding Ourselves: Breadwinning, Babies, and Bargaining Power*. New York: Basic Books, 1995.

Maushart, Susan. *The Mask of Motherhood: How Becoming a Mother Changes Everything and Why We Pretend it Doesn't*. New York: New Press, 1999.

Norwood, Robin. *Daily Meditations for Women Who Love Too Much*. New York: Tarcher/Putnum, 1997.

Orenstein, Peggy. *Flux: Women on Sex, Work, Love, Kids, and Life in a Half-Changed World*. New York: Doubleday, 2000.

Schwartz, Pepper. *Peer Marriage: How Love Between Equals Really Works*. New York: Free Press, 1994.

Taylor, Maurice and Seana McGee. *The New Couple: Why the Old Rules Don't Work and What Does*. San Francisco: HarperSanFrancisco, 2000.

Williams, Joan. *Unbending Gender: Why Family and Work Conflict and What to Do about It*. New York: Oxford University Press, 2000.

Wolf, Naomi. *Misconceptions: Truth, Lies, and the Unexpected on the Journey to Motherhood*. New York: Doubleday, 2001.

Yalom, Marilyn. *A History of the Wife*. New York: HarperCollins, 2001.

Young, Cathy. *Ceasefire! Why Women and Men Must Join Forces to Achieve True Equality*. New York: Free Press, 1994.

Levant, Ronald F. *Masculinity Reconstructed: Changing the Rules of Manhood at Work, in Relationships, and in Family Life*. New York: Dutton, 1995.

Index

F